Eruption!

VOLCANOES AND THE SCIENCE OF SAVING LIVES

Text by Elizabeth Rusch

Photographs by Tom Uhlman

Houghton Mifflin Books for Children
Houghton Mifflin Harcourt
Boston New York 2013

To the members of the Volcano Disaster Assistance Program, past, present, and future. You risk your lives to save others. Thank you.
— E.R.

Text copyright © 2013 by Elizabeth Rusch
Photographs © 2013 by Tom Uhlman

Houghton Mifflin Books for Children is an imprint of Houghton Mifflin Harcourt Publishing Company.
www.hmhbooks.com
Book design by YAY! Design.
Maps by Rachel Newborn
The text of this book is set in Bell Gothic.

Library of Congress Cataloging-in-Publication Data
Rusch, Elizabeth.
Eruption! : volcanoes and the science of saving lives / text by Elizabeth Rusch ; photographs by Tom Uhlman.
p. cm. — (Scientists in the field)
ISBN 978-0-547-50350-9
1. Volcanic eruptions—Juvenile literature. I. Uhlman, Tom, ill. II. Title.
QE521.3.R86 2013
363.34'95—dc23
2012034055

Printed in China
SCP 10 9 8 7 6 5 4 3 2 1
4500399371

Photo Credits

Jesse Allen/NASA: 43
Juan C. Alzate: iv
Associated Press: 4 (bottom)
Adek Berry/AFP/ Getty Images: 55 (bottom)
BPPTK: 37 (top right), 39, 42, 44, 46, 50 (bottom), 53, 54, 58
Corbis: 13 (left), 16
Jesus Dagmag/AFP/Getty Images: 22
Alberto P. Garcia: 27
German Aerospace Center (DLR): 49, 51 (left)
Getty Images: 5
Rick Hoblitt/USGS: 23 (right)
Houghton Mifflin Harcourt: 36 (right)
Ulet Ifansasti/Getty Images: 55 (top)
Martin LeFevers/USGS: 34
Carlos Julio Martinez/AFP/Getty Images: 1
Wendy McCausland/USGS: 20 (seismograms)
Steven M. McNally/USAF: 23 (left)
Photodisk/Getty Images: 13 (right)
Christopher Pillitz/Getty: 5
Mike Poland/USGS: 9
Claro Prima/AFP/Getty Images: 47
Reuters/Beawiharta: 52
Roger Ressmeyer/Corbis: 11
Reuters/Corbis, Clara Cortes: 18
Elizabeth Rusch: 60, 62, 73 (bottom)
STF/ATP/Getty Images: 4 (top)
Jane Sweeney/Getty Images: 2
USGS: 3 (bottom), 7, 14, 15, 17, 21, 24, 25, 26, 30 (right)
Tom Uhlman: i, 6, 28, 30 (left), 32, 33, 35 (top), 37, 38, 40, 41, 45, 48, 50 (top), 51 (right), 53 (inset), 56, 57, 59, 61, 63–71, 73 (top)
Wikipedia Commons: 3 (top)

Contents

A Note About Measurement

People in most of the world, and almost all scientists, use the metric system to describe measurements.

In this book, when measurements are given as part of a quotation in metric, we have left them in metric.

I provide both metric and United States customary for all other measurements.

The volcano Nevado del Ruiz in Colombia.

CHAPTER ONE

Sleeping Giant

On the northern tip of the Andes Mountains in Colombia, the majestic Nevado del Ruiz rises 17,680 feet (5,389 meters) into the sky, its summit draped year-round with snow and ice. To the people in its shadow, the volcano is remote and silent. Nevado del Ruiz lies dormant (inactive) for such long stretches of time that people forget it's a volcano. They should not forget.

1595

There came from this volcano such a loud, hoarse, and extraordinary thunderclap . . . [Nevado del Ruiz] hurled out a large amount of pumice, as big as ostrich eggs . . . sparkling red like iron from the forge. The [river] . . . ran so full of ash that it looked more like a thick soup of cinder than like water. Both [rivers] overflowed their channels leaving the land over which they flowed so devastated that for many years afterward it produced nothing but small weeds.
—Father Pedro Simón, a Spanish missionary

More than 630 people died following this devastating eruption, mostly members of a native tribe.

Many indigenous tribes live high on the flanks of volcanoes. This family lives near Huila in Colombia, a volcano that also unleashes deadly mudflows.

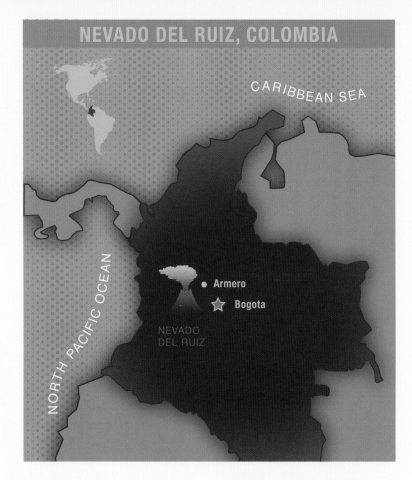

NEVADO DEL RUIZ, COLOMBIA

CARIBBEAN SEA

NORTH PACIFIC OCEAN

● Armero
☆ Bogota

NEVADO DEL RUIZ

Volcanic ash from eruptions fertilizes coffee fields near Nevado del Ruiz.

Locals eventually discovered that the area blanketed with mud and ash by the eruption was incredibly fertile. Farmers moved onto the old volcanic mudflows, planting rice and coffee. A village sprang up on the banks of the Rio Lagunillas, forty-five miles (72 kilometers) from the volcano. While Nevado del Ruiz slept, the population grew to nearly one thousand people.

1845 (250 years later)

The volcano erupted again, entombing the village and all of its residents under twenty-six feet (8 meters) of volcanic mud. The entire population perished.

Still, a few decades later, people flocked once again to the river valley. Farms thrived and businesses blossomed. Families settled the new town of Armero by the thousands. Nevado del Ruiz loomed large but lovely over the valley. Eventually, the town of Armero became home to more than thirty thousand people.

1984 (139 years later)

After more than a century of peaceful dormancy, Nevado del Ruiz began quaking with tremors, some lasting half an hour. Steam poured out of cracks, and the volcano spit ash, turning the snow on the summit gray. A new, small crater (a bowl blasted by the steam explosions) appeared inside the summit's original crater. Earthquakes continued on and off for ten months.

But all of this happened far away from Armero—forty-five miles (72 kilometers) away. To the villagers, it seemed like a safe distance.

Then one day, the volcano tossed steam into the sky for seven hours. Hot water and ash melted some snow. A small mudflow, or lahar, rolled downstream, taking out a road. But the road was on the western side, around the volcano from Armero, so the villagers didn't worry. Surely, they thought, the volcano was no threat.

Some local scientists worried about the risk, but the area newspaper *La Patria* reported on its front page, "Ruiz activity is not dangerous."

The hulking volcano continued quaking in the distance for two more months.

November 13, 1985

At 3 p.m. on the rainy afternoon of November 13, Nevado del Ruiz blasted ash into the sky again and again and again. For the first time, villagers felt the ground shaking. They got nervous, asking each other if they should leave.

Just two hours later, rain-sodden ash began to shower down on Armero. Animals paced in their pens. Dogs barked. Some people started gathering their belongings into bags and baskets.

Don't panic, stay in your houses, Radio Armero announced. The village priest echoed the message over the church's public address system.

At 7:30 that night, the earthquakes and steam eruptions calmed. The ash fall stopped. Villagers breathed a sigh of relief. Happy the worst seemed to be over, families ate dinner, checked on their animals, and tucked in their children.

Then at 9:30, Nevado del Ruiz unleashed a fury, quaking and spewing hot ash. Strong explosions lit the rain clouds over the volcano like a lamp. Masses of scorching magma (melted rock and gases)—hotter than 1,650 degrees Fahrenheit—erupted from the volcano.

Blistering clouds of searing gases, ash, and rock (called pyroclastic surges) swept across the summit of the volcano, flash-melting massive amounts of snow. Thick, ashy mud, slabs of ice, and huge rocks tore down the steep slope and avalanched into rivers.

But Nevado del Ruiz was cloaked in dark and rain.

This view of snow-covered Nevado del Ruiz was taken from Manizales City in Colombia.

Nevado del Ruiz smoked and steamed above Armero for almost a year.

3

An aerial view of the town of Armero submerged under volcanic mudflows generated from the eruption of Nevado del Ruiz.

A rescue worker frees a victim of the mudflow in Armero. She later gave birth to a child, but her husband and two other children perished in the mudflow.

Forty-five miles away (72 kilometers), villagers didn't even know the volcano had erupted.

The mudflow surged downvalley and picked up speed, approaching thirty miles (50 kilometers) per hour. A 130-foot (40-meter) wall of yellow mud ripped out the sides of the mountain and swept up boulders as big as buses. As the mass of mud neared Armero, it ROARED.

A firefighter blew his whistle and screamed: EVACUATE! EVACUATE! MOVE TO HIGHER GROUND!

But it was too late.

At 11:35 p.m., as Radio Armero played cheerful music, a towering wave of mud and rocks bulldozed through the village, roaring like a squadron of fighter jets. "We started hearing the noise in the air, like something toppling, falling, and we didn't hear anything else, no alarm," said a visitor, José Luis Restrepo.

The mudflow spread and slowed to twenty-five miles (40 kilometers) per hour. But it didn't slow enough. People ran, but they couldn't outrun the surging, hot, cementlike mud.

"We were running and about to reach the corner when a river of water came down the streets," José Luis recalled. "We turned around screaming, toward the hotel, because already the waters were dragging beds along, overturning cars, sweeping people away.

"We lost control because we saw that horrible sea of mud, which was so gigantic. . . . There were people buried, calling out, calling for help, and if one tried to go to them, one would sink into the mud."

Volcanic mudflow from the eruption of Nevado del Ruiz completely buried the town of Armero in up to fifteen feet (4.6 meters) of mud. All roads, bridges, and telephone, power, and water lines were destroyed. Sixty percent of the town's farm animals perished. More than 5,000 homes, 340 businesses, 50 schools, and 2 hospitals were wiped out.

Three-quarters of the townspeople—more than 23,000 people—died.

Armero was no longer a mountain town, but a mortuary.
Did this horrible tragedy have to happen?
Could those 23,000 lives have been saved?

A handful of U.S. Geological Survey scientists felt the answers to these questions deep in their bones.
Something could have been done.
Something *must* be done.

Children visit the graves of victims of the eruption of Nevado del Ruiz.

When Mount St. Helens erupted in
May 1980, ash shot so high into
the sky that it encircled the globe.

CHAPTER TWO

Never Again

W hen USGS geologists at the Cascades Volcano Observatory in Vancouver, Washington, saw footage of the corpses and struggling, mud-covered survivors of Armero, they were horrified. The scientists believed they could prevent tragedies like Nevado del Ruiz. Mount St. Helens, a volcano less than fifty miles from their offices, had taught them how.

Ever since Mount St. Helens erupted explosively in 1980, blasting ash into the sky, mowing down forests of huge trees like toothpicks, sending a giant mudflow fifty miles (80 kilometers) downstream to the Columbia River, and killing fifty-seven people, volcanologists had been crawling all over the crater, learning how to take the pulse of an active volcano. They hiked the ash- and boulder-strewn flanks to bury instruments that would measure earthquakes. They grabbed gas samples from the steaming crater. They surveyed the crater, looking for growing

After Mount St. Helens erupted in 1980, it became a national monument and laboratory for volcanologists to study active volcanoes. Mount St. Helens erupted on and off in the 1980s and again from 2004 to 2008.

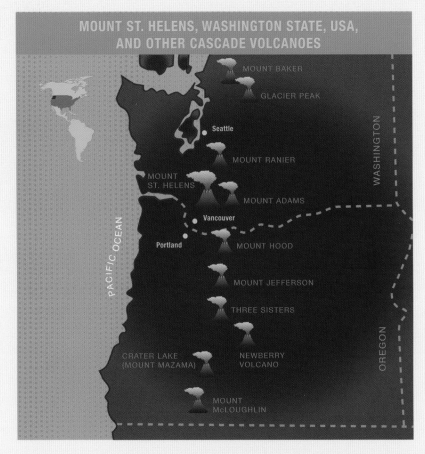

cracks and bulges. And they studied deposits from the eruption—from ash falls, pyroclastic flows, and mudflows—to better understand them.

The experience gave them incredible insight into what happens before, during, and after an eruption. The biggest lesson they learned: Volcanoes generally announce when they may erupt—hours, days, even weeks ahead of time.

"There was nothing anyone could do to *prevent* the eruption at Nevado del Ruiz," said USGS scientist Andy Lockhart. "But with the knowledge we have now, we could have read the signs and effectively warned people that the volcano was about to erupt. That horrible tragedy should never happen again."

Unless something was done, Andy and other scientists realized,

volcanic eruptions like Nevado del Ruiz would kill again. It was not a matter of *if;* it was a matter of *when*.

Andy, a compact, energetic geologist who loves international travel, recounts the frightening numbers that haunt many volcanologists. More than 1,500 potentially active volcanoes dot the globe. More than fifty volcanoes erupt each year.

More than one billion people—about 20 percent of the world's population—live where volcanic eruptions can reach them. Every year, about a dozen eruptions close to populated areas endanger people's lives.

"Volcanoes don't just erupt on desert islands, in steaming jungles, or in remote parts of the United States," said Andy, who is fascinated by volcanoes but also fears them. "There are hundreds of millions of people around the planet who live in volcano hazard zones where they could lose their homes or their lives. They need fair warning before an eruption so they can get out of the way."

A year after Armero, Andy became one of the earliest members of the first and only international volcano crisis team, called the Volcano Disaster Assistance Program. VDAP's mission was clear. This small team of scientists would bring cutting-edge equipment and knowledge to communities threatened by menacing volcanoes all over the globe to predict eruptions and prevent tragedies.

Andy and the other team members didn't know for sure if they would be successful. "We'd be landing in dangerous volcanic situations with little information about what the volcanoes had done before," said Andy. "We might not speak the native language or be familiar with the country's culture. We might not have reliable electricity, safe transportation, or even basic medical care."

And that was just the beginning of their worries.

"Even in the best of situations, forecasting if and when a volcano will erupt is incredibly tricky," said Andy.

The team would have to figure out:

Will the volcano actually erupt?

If so, when will it erupt?

How will the volcano erupt? Gentle lava flow? Powerful, destructive ash blast?

How big will the eruption be? Will blistering ash, gases, and mud reach outside the crater, down the flanks, into the countryside villages—all the way to a city?

Where will the ash, rocks, gases, and mudflows go? Is the danger on the north or south side of the volcano? Or all around?

At each volcanic crisis, the scientists would have only one chance to get it right. Andy and his colleagues knew that most people are only willing to be evacuated once. If nothing happens, locals might ignore future warnings.

"Are we going to be heroes or colossal goats in the end?" Dave Harlow, one of the team members, wondered. "You're driven and motivated by saving lives, and at the same time you don't want to make people miserable for nothing."

"Evacuations hold their own dangers," Andy explained. "Very old people, very young babies, and very sick people can suffer and even die from the stress of an evacuation. Still, we have to try to be decisive. If we don't correctly forecast an eruption and officials don't evacuate, thousands of people could die."

USGS scientist Dan Dzurisin at a Global Positioning System (GPS) station on the east flank of Mount St. Helens. Scientists have developed ways to use GPS to monitor ground swelling on volcanoes. (Mount Adams, another Cascade volcano, is visible in the distance.)

DANGER, DANGER

Volcanoes produce a dizzying variety of hazards that can kill people and destroy property. Volcanoes can produce . . .

LAVA BOMBS: Solid rock fragments hurled from a volcano with tremendous force. These deadly flying objects can hit as far as five miles (8 kilometers) from a volcano.

ERUPTION COLUMNS AND ASH CLOUDS: Fragments of volcanic glass and minerals sometimes form huge eruption columns that reach higher than twenty-five miles (40 kilometers) in less than half an hour.

AIRPLANE HAZARDS: Airborne volcanic ash can clog airplane engines, damage navigation equipment, and scrape pilots' windows so badly that they cannot see. More than eighty jets have been damaged by ash clouds in the last twenty years, and several have nearly crashed because of engine failure.

ASH FALL: What goes up must come down. Ash can completely bury the area surrounding a volcano, even spreading thousands of miles from an eruption. Heavy ash fall collapses buildings, and even minor ash fall damages crops, electronics, and machinery.

TOXIC VOLCANIC GASES: Carbon dioxide sometimes spills down the sides of a volcano, gets trapped in low areas, and suffocates people and animals. Fluorine absorbed into ash can poison grazing livestock and contaminate local water supplies. Sulfur dioxide blasting from an eruption that mixes with water droplets creates a scorching mist of sulfuric acid (called acid rain) that can burn people, corrode buildings, and destroy vegetation.

LAVA FLOWS: Molten rock, or magma, that pours or oozes onto the earth's surface is called lava. Erupting lava may form fast-moving lava streams or may spread out in broad, thin sheets as much as several miles wide.

PYROCLASTIC FLOWS: High-speed avalanches of ash, rock fragments, and gas as hot as 2,000 degrees Fahrenheit (1,095° Celsius) race down a volcano as fast as one hundred miles (160 kilometers) per hour, pummeling and burning everything in their paths.

VOLCANIC LANDSLIDE (DEBRIS AVALANCHE): Eruptions, heavy rainfall, or large earthquakes sometimes cause rocks, snow, and ice—and even entire summits or sides of a volcano—to break free and slide downhill.

MUDFLOWS OR LAHARS: One of the most deadly volcanic hazards? Mud. Hot molten rock and ash can quickly melt massive amounts of snow and ice, starting a torrent of mud powerful enough to rip up and carry trees, houses, and huge boulders more than fifty miles (80 kilometers) downstream. Lahars carry so much debris that they look like raging floods of wet concrete. When they finally stop, they entomb everything in mud.

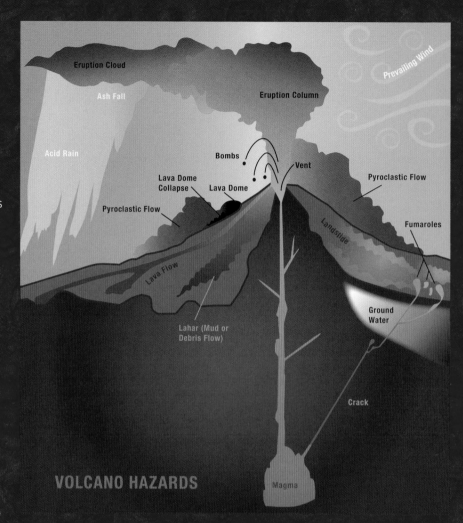

Eruption Cloud
Prevailing Wind
Ash Fall
Eruption Column
Acid Rain
Bombs
Vent
Pyroclastic Flow
Lava Dome Collapse
Lava Dome
Pyroclastic Flow
Fumaroles
Landslide
Lava Flow
Ground Water
Lahar (Mud or Debris Flow)
Crack
VOLCANO HAZARDS
Magma

CHAPTER THREE

Mount Pinatubo

USGS volcanologist Chris Newhall takes soil, water, and gas samples inside a volcano crater.

VDAP scientists got busy quickly, flying in to monitor rumbling volcanoes in Guatemala, Mexico, Bolivia, Ecuador, Argentina, Peru, and Chile over the next few years. But in April 1991, the team would get a call that would test them as never before.

Ray Punongbayan, head of the Philippine Institute of Volcanology and Seismology, called VDAP geologist Chris Newhall to report that a mountain northwest of Manila had shot steam high into the sky. Chris and Ray were friends from when Chris served in the Peace Corps in the Philippines.

A fissure a half mile (0.8 kilometer) in length had opened at the mountain's summit, and steam poured from several large fumaroles. This volcanic activity surprised everyone in the neighboring villages and the nearby U.S. military outpost, Clark Air Base. People had never seen Mount Pinatubo erupt or heard about it erupting in the past. They thought Pinatubo was a massive jungle-covered mountain—not a volcano. "The ones that have been sleeping the longest and are the poorest known are potentially the most serious ones," Chris said.

Chris and Ray knew that if Pinatubo launched a massive explosive eruption, many people would be in grave danger. More than a hundred thousand people lived on the flanks of Mount Pinatubo, with more than a million in surrounding areas.

So Chris rallied geologists Andy Lockhart and John Power, packed thirty-five trunks of equipment, and flew halfway around the world to find out more about this grumbling volcano.

When they landed at 4:00 a.m. in Manila, it was already a steamy 92° Fahrenheit (34° C) outside. Bumping along in their truck from the airport, they passed rice fields dotted with water buffalo and saw farmers in shorts, sandals, and conical straw hats. They passed Angeles City, a vibrant, crowded urban area with more than 300,000 residents. Then they drove onto Clark Air Base. With its Pizza Hut and Baskin Robbins, the base was like a slice of America in the middle of the tropics.

The team snagged an apartment on the base with a view of Pinatubo and unpacked. Later, they posted a sign: PINATUBO VOLCANO OBSERVATORY: SHAKE AND BAKE WITH THE BEST.

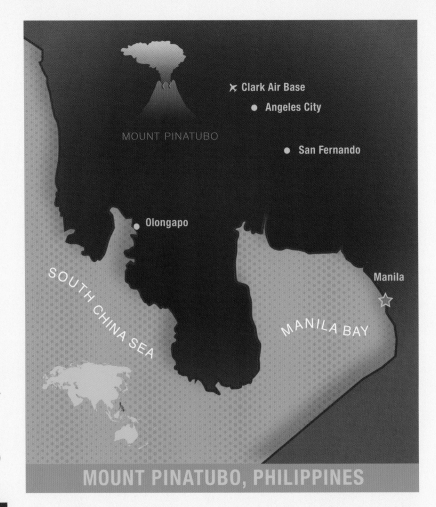

MOUNT PINATUBO, PHILIPPINES

How VDAP Works

The Volcano Disaster Assistance Program is a partnership between the U.S. Agency for International Development's Office of Foreign Disaster Assistance and the U.S. Geological Survey. VDAP's mission is to prevent international volcano crises from becoming disasters.

VDAP scientists don't swoop into volcanic crises unannounced like Indiana Jones. The team must be formally invited by a nation's government. They don't work in the limelight—they work in the background. They don't work alone, either; they partner with local scientists and confer with local officials. And finally, VDAP scientists don't order evacuations. Each country has its own process for evacuating people. VDAP's real job is narrow, clear, and incredibly difficult: to help locals predict when and how a volcano might erupt.

Wearing jeans, hiking boots, and already-sweat-drenched T-shirts, the American volcanologists and their Filipino colleagues headed out with pickaxes and buckets seeking quarries, road cuts, and river valleys where rock layers would be exposed. Not far from the base, they stopped their Chevy Suburban and piled out. Rising up before them was a canyon with walls 230 feet (70 meters) high.

"Hooooooly mooooley," said Chris. "Look at the size of these deposits." He was talking about debris from earlier volcanic eruptions. The wall had a dozen distinct layers, not of rock but of ash, mud, and pumice (rock puffed up with volcanic gases). Some layers were as thick as thirty feet (9 meters).

Farmers plant seedlings in a rice paddy.

Manila and Angeles City are full of lively open-air markets.

And they were so far from the summit of the volcano. The scientists knew there was only one way for that much ash to get that far from a volcano—sometime in the past, Pinatubo must have had some *huge* eruptions.

For three weeks, the scientists visited more than two dozen sites around Pinatubo. With the help of maps, aerial photos, and aerial flights, Chris, Andy, and John discovered that massive areas had been hit by pyroclastic flows (surges of superheated volcanic gases and ash), mudflows, and heavy ash fall. Their hazard assessment boiled down to this: Pinatubo had erupted about every thousand years, give or take five hundred years. With the last eruption six hundred years ago, the volcano was in range for another.

Even scarier, every time the volcano erupted, it was *big*. Clearly an eruption here would not consist of slowly bubbling lava like in Hawaii. A blast from Pinatubo would strip the jungle, unleash burning pyroclastic flows with hurricane force, and send out thick waves of mudflows that could sweep houses, animals, and whole villages away.

Andy and the rest of the team needed to know more about what was going on with the volcano now. They arranged for a helicopter and piled their instruments inside. It was stiflingly hot, so they strapped themselves to their seats and flew with the doors open, the wind roaring, the blades chopping overhead. Andy scanned the jungle below, searching for openings where they could land the helicopter and install seismographs to monitor earthquakes.

VDAP scientists used Clark Air Base helicopters to monitor Mount Pinatubo. Andy Lockhart, left.

He spotted a grassy green ridge. It looked perfect. The helicopter hovered closer.

It was not ordinary grass. It was elephant grass—ten feet tall. No helicopter could land in that.

"Get a little closer and I'll jump," Andy yelled to the pilot, gesturing to be sure he was understood. Andy was young and skinny, but strong. The helicopter inched closer and hovered. Andy leapt into the spiky grass, onto the volcano. The helicopter flew off.

Silence.

Andy had brought one instrument with him, a long-handled shovel. He swung the shovel at the base of the grass, hacking at it like a scythe, fighting the jungle to make a place for the helicopter to land.

"In the tall grass, the heat and the humidity are just a palpable force," Andy said. "It's like being under water. You just get a physical sense of resistance against everything you're doing. It's so hot, the first thing you've got to do is think about how hot it is. You never stop thinking about how hot it is. At some point, you start thinking, *I bet*

Shake, Shake, Shake

Earthquakes are the best clues that a volcano is stirring. As magma rises, it pushes and breaks rock, literally shaking the ground with its power. The seismograph moves with the ground when it shakes and records the movement. The squiggly line it makes is called a seismogram.

this is really dangerous. I wonder what I can do to keep from dying here."

After about an hour, the helicopter returned and landed. The team unloaded the seismograph, a garbage can, a couple of car batteries, wire, boxes, radio antennas, fifty pounds of cement, water, shovels, and a machete, purchased from a souvenir shop on the base. Andy and his colleagues dug a ditch, wired the seismograph to the batteries and antennas, sealed them in the garbage can, and buried them in the ditch. They dug trenches for the cables leading to the radio mast, which they set in the ground with concrete. The work took hours.

Andy and the team installed about one station every two days,

until they had installed seven stations all around the volcano. When seismic data started coming in, the team had a surprise. The earthquakes weren't occurring under the volcano; they were about three miles (5 kilometers) off to the northwest. The volcanologists didn't know what that meant.

On May 13, Chris lashed a sixty-pound gas-measuring instrument called a COSPEC onto a helicopter and instructed the pilot to fly in circles, low, around Pinatubo to search for volcanic gases. Magma pushing up from deep in the earth could be the source of the vigorous earthquakes and steaming cracks, known as fumaroles. Scientists needed gas clues to know for sure.

Andy Lockhart digs a hole to install seismographs on Mount Pinatubo.

Filipino scientists install monitoring stations on Mount Pinatubo.

Many of the people and animals who lived on the flanks of Mount Pinatubo were unaware of the danger threatened by the volcano.

Clark Air Base was home to nearly 2,000 houses, schools, and stores and hundreds of millions of dollars' worth of equipment, including jets like this F-15 getting ready for takeoff.

To be able to accurately identify the volcanic gas sulfur dioxide (SO_2), the COSPEC had to be under the gas plume and pointed straight up to the sky. The lower they could fly, the better the reading would be. But the danger of crashing or being blasted by an eruption would also be greater.

As the helicopter passed through the plume, the needle on the instrument danced. Mount Pinatubo was releasing five hundred tons (454 metric tons) of sulfur dioxide a day, a relatively small amount. Still, it was clear evidence that magma was on the move and getting closer to the surface.

Was that enough information to raise a warning? After all, between the air force base and the villages, hundreds of thousands lives could be in danger.

Geologists showed base commanders the seismograms, the gas

data, and their hazard maps. They presented a hair-raising video of the most dangerous volcanic hazards: pyroclastic flows and lahars.

The commanders didn't know whether to believe the ragtag group of scientists. How could that bump of a mountain off in the distance threaten the base?

So the volcanologists held a barbecue. They served hot dogs, hamburgers, and strong volcanic warnings. Chris started chatting with officers: Did they know that the entire base was built on pyroclastic flows?

"What is a pyroplastic flow?" one officer asked.

"Not pyro*plastic*—pyro*clastic*," said Chris. He went on to give a vivid description of the searing ash clouds that can roll down the side of an erupting volcano at speeds of one hundred miles (160 kilometers) per hour. At 2,000° Farenheit (1,000° C), they wipe out everything in their path.

"So what you're telling me," said the officer, "is that in a big eruption it's possible that the people living on the base could be toast?"

That was exactly what the volcanologists were telling him.

Mount Pinatubo emits steam and volcanic gases.

Sniffing Out the Gas

Why do scientists search the air around a volcano for volcanic gases? Imagine a bottle of soda that you've shaken but haven't opened. It's full of gas ready to fizz out. But you don't see many bubbles because the gas is under pressure. Magma under the earth is like the soda. It's a mixture of liquid (melted rock) and gas under high pressure.

As magma pushes up a volcano's vent, it's like that hiss you hear when you open a soda bottle. The pressure drops and some gas escapes. At a restless volcano, gas may escape in a slow leak at first. But when gassy magma nears the surface, the volcano can really pop. Expanding gas provides the force that can blast lava and ash explosively out of a volcano.

Geologists looking for signs that a volcano may erupt search for at least three kinds of gases: carbon dioxide, hydrogen sulfide, and sulfur dioxide. Large quantities of volcanic gas usually suggest a large magma chamber below the volcano. And the more gas that the magma contains, the larger and more explosive the eruption might be.

Angelito Lamida, a Filipino volcanologist, monitors earth movements using a seismograph inside Clark Air Base near Mount Pinatubo.

CHAPTER FOUR

To Evacuate or Not to Evacuate?

On May 28, Chris got a new gas reading from Mount Pinatubo. Sulfur dioxide (SO_2) had jumped tenfold, to 5,000 tons a day. The volcano was definitely ramping up.

A few days later, instruments recorded two unusual earthquakes. A shallow, continuous, rhythmic shaking known as a low-frequency earthquake meant magma was moving toward the surface and releasing more gas. Then the seismographs recorded the first earthquake directly under the vent.

Over the next few weeks, the volcano spat steam higher and higher into the sky. The plume changed color from white to gray. Then the volcano began shooting rock and ash. But the geologists tested the ash and found no sign of fresh lava. The steam explosions were just tossing up old material. Would the volcano erupt, or would it just spit steam until it slipped back into dormancy?

Then the sulfur dioxide plummeted, from 5,000 tons to 1,300 to 260 a day. That could mean the volcano was settling down.

Or . . . it could mean the volcano's vent was clogged, with pressure building.

Andy and the other scientists watched the seismograph around the clock. They saw bigger quakes, longer quakes, and a harmonic tremor, a constant humming earthquake that often means magma is rising and boiling away groundwater.

The Americans and Filipinos each had their own alert level systems. The VDAP scientists debated. Was it time to raise the alert level to three: high and increasing unrest; eruption possible in two weeks?

Ray, the head of the Filipino geologists, would need time to spread any warning to people scattered in villages all around Pinatubo. He raised his alert level to three: eruption possible in two weeks. About 10,000 members of the Aeta tribes were moved to evacuation camps.

The quakes accelerated. Magma moving all along the conduit was

An Eruption Unfolds, Earthquake by Earthquake

VDAP scientists and their colleagues have studied the earthquakes preceding many eruptions. They have noticed a pattern that may suggest that a volcano is heading toward an eruption. Every volcano crisis is different, but here's how volcanic eruptions often unfold:

DISTAL VOLCANO TECTONIC EARTHQUAKES

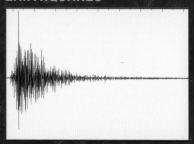

Often the first earthquakes detected near a volcano, sometimes long before an eruption, are similar to tectonic earthquakes along preexisting tectonic faults. They happen near, rather than right under, a volcano at early stages. This suggests that pressure underground is stressing nearby fault zones and breaking brittle rock in the area around the volcano. Tectonic earthquakes located under the volcano suggest that the pressure has become focused closer to the vent, or opening, of the volcano.

HYBRID EARTHQUAKES

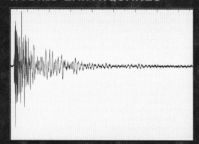

When a volcano begins to ramp up toward an eruption, there is often a mixture of different earthquakes associated with different processes: volcano tectonic earthquakes that represent the breaking of rock; low-frequency earthquakes associated with the movement of fluids (gases, liquids, or magma); and hybrid earthquakes that start like a tectonic earthquake and become low-frequency, which may represent rock breaking and fluid movement.

EXPLOSION SIGNAL

Before a volcano actually erupts magma, it will usually first erupt gases and steam into the air. These steam explosions suggest that the vent has been at least partially blasted open.

EARTHQUAKES UNDER THE VOLCANO

Within days of the steam eruptions, the largest distal volcano tectonic earthquakes occur. Then they tend to diminish. Earthquakes now center mostly under the volcano and are usually low-frequency or hybrid.

LOW-FREQUENCY EARTHQUAKES

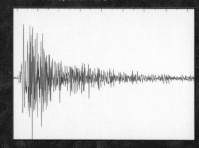

Large amounts of gases and liquids surging though cracks and vents underground shake the ground in a very different way from when brittle rock breaks. Earthquakes associated with magma and gas rising to the surface are lower-frequency, meaning there is more time between an upswing and downswing on a seismogram.

REPETITIVE EARTHQUAKES

During some eruptions, hybrid earthquakes can become evenly spaced, and similarly sized. These repetitive earthquakes could occur when a plug of magma surges slowly but steadily up to the vent. Or they could be the result of pulses of gas from the magma opening and closing cracks underground. Repetitive earthquakes can lead to a nonexplosive dome-building eruption or an explosive eruption. It all depends on how fast the magma rises and whether the conduit is open enough for the magma to move through—or is clogged with pressure building.

TREMOR

A long-lasting, rhythmic seismic signal, called a tremor, is a common precursor to an eruption.

BIGGER, MORE NUMEROUS EARTHQUAKES

When earthquakes that are steady or slowly increasing in size or number have a marked increase in the size and number, this means one thing: The volcano is going to blow! Time to evacuate!

The more slowly a volcano moves through these steps, the more time is available for gas to leak out without exploding. A rapid ramp-up, at any time, usually means a bigger, more explosive eruption.

shaking the ground deep in the earth and quite near the surface. More and more steam and ash poured from cracks in the volcano, called fumaroles.

The volcanologists estimated the size of the magma chamber (the reservoir of melted rock and gas under the volcano) and the potential size of the eruption. The eruption could be ten times larger than the 1980 eruption of Mount St. Helens, which was bigger than any living geologist had ever seen.

Military officers listened intently to the geologists' briefings. At the end of one, Major General William Studer asked: What would you do?

The scientists answered: Move the dependents off the base.

The officers relocated pregnant women and the elderly. The air force newspaper and TV station began broadcasting details of an evacuation plan: what to bring and where to go.

The earthquakes got even closer to the surface. A steam plume reached 28,000 feet (8,500 meters), the highest so far.

After conferring with VDAP scientists, Ray raised his alert to level four, enlarging the evacuation zone for the local population. Filipinos all around the volcano packed a few possessions and walked or rode carts down the mountain.

VDAP members debated: Should we move to level four? The air force had set VDAP's level four as a trigger for Clark to be evacuated. Evacuating 14,000 people and millions of dollars of equipment would be a huge challenge, and a huge burden to the military and their families.

Some VDAP members thought they should.

Then the earthquakes diminished.

"Volcanoes don't necessarily move from deep sleep to violent eruption in a straight, orderly progression," Andy said. "They ramp up and drop down, ramp up and drop down. The trend at Pinatubo was

Mount Pinatubo steams behind an air force helicopter.

ramping higher and dropping down less. Any single episode of ramping up could lead to a full-blown eruption. But it could all just peter out to nothing." The scientists had to predict the unpredictable. The consequences—a costly false evacuation or tragic loss of life—weighed heavily on their minds and their hearts.

On June 8, a chopper lifted off to give scientists a closer view of the summit. The sky cleared. They could see that a big, ugly gray blob of rock had poked out of the east crater wall. It was a lava dome. Cold, hard, heavy rock could be clogging the vent. With magma moving up with nowhere to go and pressure building, this thing could blow—with deadly results.

The scientists told the air force commanders the new development and waited for them to take action.

Then, the next morning, June 9, when Andy and his colleague hopped into the helicopter, it took a detour—to the center of the base.

Looking for Lumps

Changes in the surface of a volcano give clues about what is happening beneath. Imagine a mole tunneling under a lawn. When the mole moves, the grass bumps up. Magma moving underground does the same thing, actually lifting the ground above it. When magma is close to the surface, the bulge can grow hundreds of feet high and hundreds of feet wide.

Lava shoved out of an erupting volcano can also make a massive bulge or dome. Domes and bulges might plug a vent, causing pressure to build underground. Domes can also grow so large that they trigger landslides. So scientists have to track their growth, too.

How do scientists measure all these lumps and bulges? Digital elevation maps—compiled using photos and radar data—show the length, width, and height of every part of the volcano. Scientists compare DEMs compiled at different times to track how the shape of the volcano has changed. They can also make these measurements using satellite radar images, GPS, meters that track how the ground tilts, or by careful surveying.

Aeta tribespeople threatened by Mount Pinatubo flee their village with their meager belongings.

General Studer and his second-in-command climbed aboard. The helicopter headed for the volcano.

Instead of billowing steam and ash, only a thin snake of yellow-gray plume drifted up from the summit.

"Geez, that's a lot of ash," the general commented.

"That's nothing," the volcanologists said. They pointed out how underlying the jungle all around the mountain were signs of massive ancient pyroclastic flows. "That's all ash from the last eruption." The helicopter turned, and the widespread devastation once wrought by this volcano became impossible to miss. The general stared silently out the window as the helicopter headed back to the base.

Finally, he turned to his second in command. "Do it tomorrow," he said.

June 10, 1991

At 6 a.m., military television and radio echoed with the order to evacuate. The streets of Clark Air Base filled with cars, trucks, and buses that funneled downhill through the shantytowns and toward a naval station an hour away. By noon, 14,500 people had evacuated.

The Filipinos extended their evacuation to twelve miles (20 kilometers), displacing 25,000 people. People with carts piled high with furniture and leading water buffalo shared the road with the long line of military trucks and the cars of people evacuating the base.

Left on the base were some officers, the Military Police (MPs), and engineers who could keep the lights on. The volcanologists moved their observatory to the farthest corner of the base. "We were just incredibly relieved that most everybody was out of the way," Andy said.

But the pressure still weighed on the scientists.

"I couldn't help second-guessing myself," said team member Dave Harlow. "All of us did. I was feeling as though the chances were pretty high that we would all be hauled in front of committees investigating the disastrous evacuation, its costs and impact to the Philippine economy and on the air force."

Would Mount Pinatubo really explode? The next few days would tell.

Andy woke up to a blue-sky morning on June 12. It was after 6 a.m., and the clouds had usually rolled in by then. But the sun shone brightly as he waited for geologist Rick Hoblitt, who was going to give Andy a lift to the observatory.

"LET'S GO!" Rick hollered from upstairs.

Geez, Andy thought. *What's up with him?*

Rick raced down the stairs, taking two at a time, just as Andy opened the front door.

A huge black ash column pumped out of the volcano, filling the sky.

"OH MY GOD!" Andy shouted. The column rose up higher and higher. Rick and Andy jumped into their truck and raced off.

By the time they got to the observatory at the edge of the base, the ash column had hit the stratosphere. The cloud mushroomed out, reaching the sky right above them.

Then the cloud slowed, stopped, and started to dissipate.

"Wahoo! Whoa! Cool!" the MPs hollered. They started doing

Military personnel and their families evacuate Clark Air Base.

Threatened by Mount Pinatubo, Clark Air Base was evacuated on June 10. The light-colored peak in the center is the summit of Pinatubo.

The June 12, 1991, eruption of Mount Pinatubo, viewed from Clark Air Base.

a victory dance, because they thought they'd just seen the eruption and survived.

But Andy and Rick didn't dance. They turned to their instruments. They knew that this could be just the beginning.

For the next few days Pinatubo shot steam, rumbled, and kept the scientists on edge. Several times, the volcano shot up columns as big as the one on June 12.

But on June 14, the volcano stopped shooting steam and ash. Pinatubo shook as much as it had two days before, but nothing came out. *The volcano is all stopped up,* Andy thought.

He fell asleep late that night, restless and worried. Then on June 15, Andy and other scientists were jolted from sleep by a cry.

GET UP! GET UP! yelled the scientist on watch.

Andy ran to the front door. Clouds obscured the top of the volcano and pelting rain blurred Andy's view. But great black ash clouds— massive, rolling clouds of superheated ash—raged down six miles (10 kilometers) on each side of the volcano.

Pyroclastic flows!

Moments later, rain and wind from a typhoon that had hit the island completely hid the erupting volcano.

Andy rushed to the seismograph.

The earthquakes died down, way down, and stayed down.

"This is bad," Andy muttered.

The pressure under the volcano was building.

"Should we evacuate?" the scientists asked each other.

The decision was quick. Someone yelled: EVACUATE THE BASE!

Everyone started moving all at once, grabbing things, yelling. Officers, MPs, and scientists piled into cars and sped away.

From a big field, they watched the dark volcano. They waited.

The volcanologists wanted to see their instruments. They wanted to find out what this volcano was up to so they could extend the evacuation zone if needed, or learn something that would help at another crisis. But that would mean risking their own lives.

They decided they'd been too hasty evacuating themselves. They drove back to the observatory on the base, along with the base commanders.

It was raining. Not just water and ash, but egg-size chunks of pumice. The scientists hurried into the building and crowded around the seismographs.

The earthquakes were so intense that the seismograph needles just banged from the top to the bottom of the drum, *TUNK, TUNK, TUNK, TUNK*, making alarming blocks of solid ink.

Pinatubo blasted ash higher and higher. The scientists watched, aghast, as monitoring stations blinked out one by one on the far side of the volcano—destroyed. Then a station went down on their side—the one in the elephant grass.

That was only twelve miles (20 kilometers) from where they were standing.

Was a searing pyroclastic flow heading their way?

Flows moved at up to one hundred miles (160 kilometers) an hour. Did the scientists have only precious moments before they themselves fell victim to an eruption like the citizens of Armero had? Not from mudflows this time, but from raging, searing pyroclastic flows?

This time the scientists knew they had no time to evacuate. They raced for the back of the building, the farthest they could get from the erupting monster.

They waited, panting, sweating.

Andy could stand it no longer. He went back to the front door. All he saw was black—complete black—from the rain, the dark clouds, the ash fall. The sound was terrifying—like a wall of rock a mile high racing down at breakneck speeds.

This ash-covered news box on Clark Air Base tells the story of the headline.

I could die, Andy thought. *All my friends could die.*

He watched and he watched, his eyes glued to a row of lights on an airstrip that pointed toward the volcano. "I figured that as long as I could see the lights, the pyroclastic flow hadn't reached us. If the lights went out, I had maybe twenty seconds to run to the back of the building. Maybe that would be enough protection. Or maybe the pyroclastic flow would peel off the roof and immolate us all."

Then the air and sky seemed to lighten, just a shade. The pyroclastic flow hadn't reached the base. Andy and his friends checked the instruments. Everything was flatlining—all the monitoring stations had been destroyed—except for one. A station on the base.

The volcanologists quickly grabbed what they could, piled into trucks, and tore off. That is, until they merged with hordes of evacuating Filipinos. "It was a huge, slow-moving traffic jam of everybody with a water buffalo strolling out of town," says Andy. "We were going crazy with the delay, but at least we were headed away from the volcano."

But Andy, the other volcanologists, and the villagers managed to escape with their lives.

The eruption of Mount Pinatubo was the second largest eruption in the twentieth century. A few hundred people died, most in buildings that later collapsed under the weight of rain-soaked ash. But more than 20,000 lives were saved. "We got it right," Andy said. "We questioned ourselves and doubted ourselves as things unfolded, but we got it right."

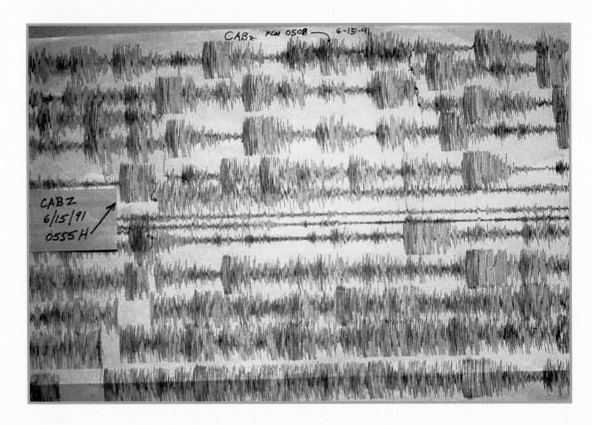

This seismogram of a two-hour period in June 15, 1991, shows the heavy seismicity accompanying the catastrophic eruption of Mount Pinatubo. The arrow points to the earthquake accompanying a major explosion just before 6 a.m., which was preceded by many large long-period earthquakes.

Pyroclastic flows surge from Mount Pinatubo
during its huge June 15, 1991, eruption.

Chilean volcanologists Gonzalo Andrés Hermosilla (left) and Luis Enrique Franco examine volcanic ash on Mount St. Helens.

CHAPTER FIVE

Volcano Training Camp

For two decades after the eruption of Mount Pinatubo, the VDAP team continued to fly to dozens of volcano crises in Central and South America, the Caribbean, Africa, Asia, and the South Pacific. Though none matched the scale of Pinatubo, the team members helped local scientists predict eruptions and save lives.

But sometimes three or four volcanoes threaten at the same time. "Volcanoes don't wait in line to erupt," Andy says.

The team has remained small, and as much as the scientists want to, they can't be everywhere at once. So when facing multiple crises, VDAP scientists have to ask some very difficult questions: How many people are at risk? How dangerous is the volcano?

The most dangerous volcanoes closest to the most people get their attention first. "When something is going on that could be bad, really bad, we help them get monitoring equipment up there, fast," Andy says.

But the scientists desperately needed to find a way to extend their reach. "We have a lot of experience forecasting different types of eruptions, so we have something to contribute

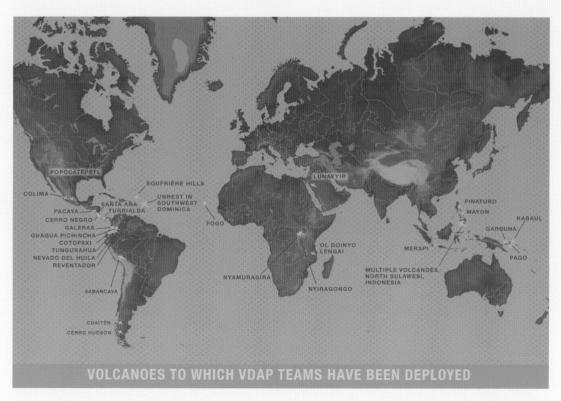

POPOCATÉPETL
COLIMA
PACAYA
CERRO NEGRO
GALERAS
GUAGUA PICHINCHA
COTOPAXI
TUNGURAHUA
NEVADO DEL HUILA
REVENTADOR
SABANCAYA
CHAITÉN
CERRO HUDSON
SANTA ANA
TURRIALBA
SOUFRIÈRE HILLS
UNREST IN SOUTHWEST DOMINICA
FOGO
NYAMURAGIRA
NYIRAGONGO
OL DOINYO LENGAI
LUNAYYIR
MERAPI
MULTIPLE VOLCANOES, NORTH SULAWESI, INDONESIA
PINATUBO
MAYON
GARBUNA
RABAUL
PAGO

VOLCANOES TO WHICH VDAP TEAMS HAVE BEEN DEPLOYED

Luis (right) and Gonzalo (left) study a seismogram from the 1980 eruption of Mount St. Helens with VDAP member Wendy McCausland.

Earthquakes felt near Chaitén on April 30, 2008, provided the first warning of increasing volcanic activity. Twenty-seven hours later, on May 2, the volcano erupted with an ash column that rose to eleven miles (17 kilometers) and lasted for six hours. Continued eruptions with nearly continuous ash emission and intermittent large explosions led to full evacuation of Chaitén. Within days, heavy rains generated lahars and wiped out the town.

during a volcano crisis in addition to equipment," says Andy. "But we can't be everywhere. What's more, we can't be as effective as local volcanologists can be. They know the area and work with the people over the long run to help them understand the volcano hazard. We decided we could bring the lessons of our experience and good equipment to local volcanologists to help them do their jobs better, and save lives."

Volcano training camp is at the Cascades Volcano Observatory, a brick building surrounded by western red cedars, in Washington State.

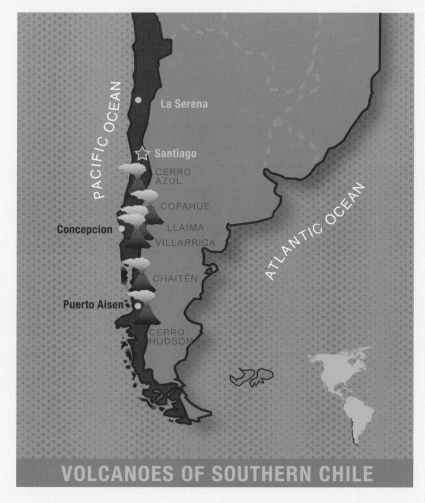

VOLCANOES OF SOUTHERN CHILE

Two Chilean volcanologists, Luis Enrique Franco and Gonzalo Andrés Hermosilla, have come to VDAP to deepen their knowledge of volcano monitoring.

In the past, Chile had only six geologists watching 122 active volcanoes. But when Chaitén erupted violently in 2008, VDAP assisted Chilean scientists and talked to the president of Chile about the importance of volcano monitoring. Inspired by VDAP's work—and USGS monitoring of the 169 potentially active U.S. volcanoes—the Chilean government greatly expanded its volcano hazards program.

Chilean volcanologists have identified their most dangerous volcanoes and have committed to setting up more than four hundred monitoring stations on forty-three volcanoes in the next five years. Only a few sites will be accessible by car. Most will require helicoptering—or worse, lugging all the equipment on their backs.

Andy and his team are quickly but carefully packing volcano monitoring equipment into shiny, weatherproof metal boxes. The VDAP scientists hope to helicopter to the upper flanks of Mount St. Helens to a remote monitoring site. The Chileans will watch, help, and learn as the Americans do maintenance on old equipment and set up the new monitoring station. If Luis and Gonzalo go through the paces with Andy and his team, they will be better prepared to assemble the many stations they need in Chile.

Twenty years after Pinatubo, Andy's still lean and fit, with a tuft of white hair and round Harry Potter–style glasses. His office looks like the workspace of an inventor. Its desk is covered with a jumble of metal scraps, tools, clamps, and a soldering iron. Spools of wires hang from the walls. This is where Andy builds, fiddles, and tinkers—unless he needs more space. Then he heads down the hall to the electronics room, run by VDAP member Marvin Couchman.

Coils of wire circle this room, thick and thin wires of red, black, white, and blue. A cabinet with scads of small drawers holds phone

VDAP member Andy Lockhart packs a seismometer into a plastic pipe to be installed at a new monitoring station on Mount St. Helens.

plugs, clips, tie downs, and connectors. There's a huge red metal toolbox, drills, vise grips, and computers with their innards hanging out.

At one of the high tables in the electronics lab, Andy and Luis pack a seismometer. Luis, slim and strong with a long face, broad forehead, and short hair on top, is actually a Colombian volcanologist working in Chile. He's been working on volcano monitoring ever since the tragedy at Nevado del Ruiz. "Never again" is a resolve that he and the VDAP scientists share.

Andy slides a seismometer into a piece of white plastic sewer pipe from the hardware store. "We try to make things out of stuff people can buy anywhere in the world," Andy comments. "We experimented with basic plumbing materials and hardware until we figured out how to make a tough waterproof case." He squirts the pipe full of silicon grease and seals it in a black cylinder.

Luis watches intently, as if Andy is turning lead into gold. "You can bury this anywhere, in a hurry if you need to," Andy says. "You can set it in the mud and it will still work."

Luis and Andy discuss the challenges of placing delicate equipment in the jungles of southern Chile. Roads are scarce in the jungle, Luis tells Andy, so he sometimes has to hike for hours carrying equipment on his back and swinging a machete to clear a path. The vegetation is so thick that radio signals won't make it through.

"And with the humidity," Luis says, "the batteries don't last as long."

They discuss the sealant. A tight seal will keep the moisture—and also insects—out. "Any little critter who gets in there will mess everything up," Luis laughs.

Andy and Luis are joined by another Chilean volcanologist, who just stepped in from a long talk with a fellow seismologist. Gonzalo, tall with large, soft brown eyes and a shock of wavy hair is single-handedly setting up a regional observatory in Patagonia to monitor volatile volcanoes such as Hudson, Maca-Cay, and Corcovado. His home base is in the small town of Coyhaique.

"I'm responsible for a whole bunch of volcanoes," he says, looking a little worried. "I want to install a whole bunch of seismometers."

Gonzalo's eagerness about the project is clear. "I want to see the installation, how to operate everything. I want to get a good example to use in our own country. I want to talk to professionals, meet people in the field. I want to talk more about different kinds of earthquakes, what makes them and what they mean," he says.

In the warehouse, shiny metal poles shaped like a swing set hold

Marvin Couchman builds much of VDAP's equipment and signs it "MC" with a felt-tip pen. Marv is known by his initials to many volcanologists who have never met him but rely on his equipment. "At volcanoes all over the world, MC means well made," Andy says.

solar panels overhead. Nearby, wires pour over the sides of metal boxes. Andy and his team assemble the monitoring station in the warehouse so they can show the Chileans how it's done. Later when they disassemble it, all that's left of the swing set contraption is a pile of equipment packed and ready to load. A helicopter will carry the gear to the top of Mount St. Helens in a sling dangling below. The team has weighed every box, every pile of poles, so each load will be less than eight hundred pounds (363 kilograms). The helicopter cannot exceed its weight limit or it will be yanked back like a dog hitting the end of its leash.

The scientists pile into a pale green USGS truck and wind their way up the highway to Mount St. Helens National Monument. Andy drives as the Chileans stare out the window, awed at the miles of massive trees slammed down like toothpicks during the 1980 eruption. They take in the gaping gray crater and the long valley that had been completely blanketed in ash and mud.

"Before the eruption there was no obvious dome?" asks Luis.

"Right, it was just a beautiful snow-covered peak," Andy explains. "The bulge that grew would have been right there." He points to where the crater wall is missing.

"The scale is so impressive," Gonzalo whispers.

He wants to know all about the debris he is seeing. "That is from the landslide? The blast? The pyroclastic flow?" he asks and gestures. "And the mudflow went all the way down there?"

Gonzalo, Wendy, and Luis (right to left) discuss the seismometers that constantly monitor earthquakes on Mount St. Helens.

VDAP members and the Chilean visitors install a new monitoring station on Mount St. Helens and repair an old one.

"To the Columbia River," Andy says.

Gonzalo whistles. He recognizes the same debris pattern from an eruption at Villarica, a Chilean volcano he has studied closely. "But this is so much bigger," he says.

The volcanologists talk about their work, about the dangers. "When you're in the crater, any small thing can kill you," Andy says. "Nowhere is safe in the crater of an active volcano." Luis and Gonzalo nod.

They continue to Johnston Ridge Visitor Center, oblivious to the hordes of tourists with their cameras. Around the side of the build-ing, Andy and the Chileans gather around an antenna cemented into the ground. Andy unlocks a metal cabinet the size of a refrigerator. He points out the components of the radio that transmits signals from monitoring stations in the crater and on the volcano's flanks to the central office in Vancouver.

A cloud passes above and it gets colder, but the Chileans aren't ready to go. They have more questions. Gonzalo stomps on the

The antenna near Johnston Ridge Visitor Center transmits signals from monitoring stations on Mount St. Helens to the Cascades Volcano Observatory.

concrete. "How big is this platform? How deep down does the foundation go?" They estimate it and discuss how much concrete would be needed for this antenna and for a taller one.

"This won't always work for us in Chile," Gonzalo says. "We don't always have a clear line of sight." The scientists talk about using satellites to relay data.

"It's a pretty new way of doing things, but in some places it's the only option," Andy says.

"Yes, I want to understand everything that went on here so I can apply what I need," Gonzalo says. Andy and his team try to teach him everything they know.

A few weeks later, in late summer 2010, VDAP scientists host two more volcanologists, from Indonesia. "As more scientists get training and our load lightens in Latin America, we have been able to turn our attention to Indonesia," says Andy. The island country in the Pacific, part of the Ring of Fire, has more than 120 active volcanoes looming over one hundred million people. "Something is always blowing up there," Andy observes.

Chris Newhall and a newer VDAP member, John Pallister, who is now the director of the program, had already begun helping Indonesian scientists build their first regional observatory. "We visited and got to know the Indonesian team. We spread maps on the floor of the observatory and talked about the hazards and made plans together. Then they visited us here at CVO to see how we do things in the United States. It's

MOUNT MERAPI, INDONESIA

Peanut M&M's and the Ring of Fire

MOUNT
ST. HELENS

MOUNT
PINATUBO

NEVADO
DEL RUIZ

MERAPI

CHAITÉN

THE PACIFIC RING OF FIRE

What does the Ring of Fire have to do with Peanut M&M's? The earth has three main layers, much like a peanut M&M. The crust, like the crunchy candy coating of the M&M, is a shell of solid rock. The mantle is like the soft chocolate, with rock so hot that it melts into thick paste. The core is like the peanut, solid metal in the center of the earth.

The earth is not exactly like an M&M, though. The crust is not all one piece. It's broken up into huge slabs, called plates, that cover the planet like a jigsaw puzzle. These plates move apart and crash together in many places.

Around the edge of the massive Pacific Plate is the most volcanically active area on earth. The so-called Ring of Fire, which includes the Philippines, Chile, Indonesia, and the Cascade volcanoes of the Pacific Northwest, has more than 450 volcanoes and is home to three-quarters of the world's active and dormant volcanoes. "The Ring of Fire keeps us—and volcanologists all over the world—very busy," Andy says.

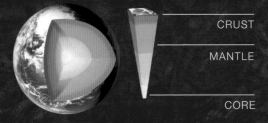

CRUST

MANTLE

CORE

this combination of scientific exchange, common goals, and diplomatic friendship building that makes it work," says John. "We know and trust each other."

Good thing, because the American and Indonesian scientists were about to face a crisis of huge proportions.

Shoulder to shoulder, the American and Indonesian scientists make an assembly line in the VDAP lab: taking electronic boards, placing chips, testing the boards, and sealing them in boxes.

"So what's up at Merapi?" Andy asks Anton, a technician from Indonesia. "I heard the alert level was raised."

"We have increased earthquakes," Anton replies. "We think it's heading toward another eruption."

Just seventeen miles (28 kilometers) north of the city of

Yogyakarta, Mount Merapi looms. Its name loosely translated as "Mountain of Fire," Mount Merapi is one of Indonesia's most active and dangerous volcanoes. Smoke snakes up from the 9,800-foot (2,987-meter) summit more than three hundred days a year, with small eruptions occurring every three to five years and larger ones every dozen years or so. A large eruption that took place about 1000 AD blanketed all of central Java with ash. The volcano also erupted violently in 1786, 1822, and 1872. In 1930, thirteen villages were destroyed and 1,400 people killed by pyroclastic flows.

Mount Merapi presides over one of the most densely populated areas in the world. More than a million people live nearby, with many villages situated right up on the flanks of the volcano, 5,600 feet (1,700 meters) above sea level.

Still, the American scientists are not overly concerned. "The general feeling is that the eruption would be like the past half dozen or so, small and affecting a fairly predictable area," John says.

But what if they're wrong?

VDAP member Julie Griswold (left) confers with Indonesian volcanologist Dewi Sri Sayudi.

VDAP member John Pallister (right) discusses lahars with Indonesian volcanologist Pak Subandrio.

Indonesian volcano Mount Merapi looms over the city of Yogyakarta on the island of Java.

Many village schools on Mount Merapi are vulnerable during an eruption.

CHAPTER SIX

How Do You Watch a Volcano You Can't See?

BRRRRING! The phone jolts John Pallister awake before 5 a.m. on the morning of October 22, 2010. It's Surono, John's friend and the head of the Center for Volcanology and Geological Hazard Mitigation (CVGHM) in Indonesia. He's calling from the observatory at Mount Merapi.

Located in the crowded city of Yogyakarta, the Mount Merapi observatory is an old two-story building with a cement central courtyard that looks like a garage with a high ceiling. Inside resembles the VDAP offices, with a geochemistry lab, lots of maps, and equipment, some of it compliments of VDAP. Badminton is the national sport of Indonesia, so the central courtyard features a badminton court. Members of the community use the court to play when things are calm. But now things are far from calm.

Surono has just taken a close look at Merapi's seismic data. He recognizes instantly that the situation is serious. The volcano's ramping up more quickly than he has ever seen, with more and bigger earthquakes than in the last dozen eruptions.

Surono, a volcanologist, heads the Center for Volcanology and Geological Hazard Mitigation in Indonesia.

"I've already gone to alert level two," Surono tells John. In Indonesia, alert level two means that the volcano is experiencing unrest and an eruption is possible.

John's heart goes out to his friend. He wishes he could fly out and help, but much of the VDAP team is in Guatemala. He's manning home base, so he can't leave.

"Keep me posted," says John. "Let me know what you learn and what we can do to help."

The hundreds of thousands of people in the hot, bustling streets of Yogyakarta are oblivious to the increasing danger of the volcano. Street vendors sell batik clothes, odd spiky fruit called durian, and thrashing live fish. Darting motorcycles carry men and women to work. A family with a mom, dad, baby, and two schoolchildren on one scooter surge forward alongside a scooter with huge bundles of elephant grass strapped to the driver's back, and another with piles of vegetables stuffed in baskets.

High up on the flanks of the volcano, things seem peaceful too. A young couple rides a motorcycle to their patch of land, where together they will till the fields, weed them, and harvest. For the day they have left their cows, chickens, ducks, and children in the village. Elementary school students—boys in clean dark blue pants and white shirts and girls in long dark blue skirts, tunics, and headscarves—gather in a dirt yard outside school for their weekly assembly. An old woman walks down the street carrying a large bundle of grass cut for their family's cow. Grandmothers with swaddled babies chat in the street.

Surono is not sure how dangerous things might be. He radios Ismail, an observer at Babadan Observatory, located just under three miles (4.4 kilometers) from the summit. The observatory is a two-bedroom house of white-painted cement with lime green trim, a small garden, and a stunning view of the jagged summit of Mount Merapi.

The picture-postcard view is for a reason. Twenty-four hours a

Villagers who live on Mount Merapi harvest grass from high on the volcano to feed their cattle.

Local volcano observer Ismail stays in close radio contact with the observatory in Yogyakarta.

A woman sells flowers at a market in downtown Yogyakarta.

day, seven days a week, observers like Ismail, people hired from the village, watch the volcano. They observe the weather, the temperature, and the way the volcano looks. They watch the seismometers for changes in the number of volcanic earthquakes. They answer questions such as:

Is the volcano smoking?

Is the steam white like normal or brown or dark or thick?

Does the smoke rise just above the crater and dissipate? Or is there more power that shoots the steam higher and straighter up to the sky?

Are there bulges that were not there before, or new cracks?

Is it raining on the summit? How much? Even between eruptions heavy rainfall can sweep up old ash and start a dangerous mudflow.

Ismail's observations are not very out of the ordinary. He trudges the steep trail up the volcano past fields of chilies, cauliflower, and cabbage for a gas sample. He slogs on through lava rocks and gray ash to the summit, a rotten egg stench sharp in his nostrils.

Ismail has been an observer for twenty years, and he notices immediately that it's hotter than normal—not from the beating sun, but from the heat of the volcano below. He bores a hole in the crater and sticks in a thermometer. It reads 580 degrees Celcius (1,076° F), almost 200 degrees hotter than usual.

Back at the observatory, Ismail radios in his report: "The smoke seemed stronger, darker somehow."

"Watch the volcano carefully," Surono signs off.

But how do you watch a volcano you cannot see? The summit of Merapi, on a good day, is visible from 6 a.m. to 9 a.m. The other

Local volcano observers and scientists take gas samples on Mount Merapi.

Local volcanologists trudge down the ash-covered slopes near the summit of Mount Merapi.

twenty-one hours it is shrouded in clouds or darkness. And Ismail and the other observers are not getting many good days.

"Here's where we can give you a hand," John tells Surono. He offers to send Surono reports of what is happening at the summit based on data from satellites. John and his colleagues at USGS offices in Washington State, Alaska, and Virginia immediately start a campaign of satellite remote sensing.

At VDAP, geologist Julie Griswold coordinates the remote sensing data and sends images to colleagues in Indonesia. Meanwhile, surveying of the volcano by the Indonesian team reveals that Mount Merapi has begun inflating on the south side, literally expanding as magma and gases pool beneath the surface.

John and Surono call, e-mail, and text each other. Everything starts happening fast. Seismographs record five hundred volcanic earthquakes in two days. Calculations suggest the magma has risen to 3,300 feet (1 kilometer) below the summit.

Julie barely has time to sleep. She gets up at 2 or 3 a.m. to gather images and data. During the day, she sorts through material with John and other colleagues. At the end of the day, the Indonesian scientists are just getting to their offices, eager for information—so she stays late to communicate with them.

On this false-color satellite image of two volcanoes in the Democratic Republic of Congo taken in 2007, the bright pink dot shows elevated surface temperatures at the summit of Nyiragongo. The bright blue haze streaming west of the vent is a plume of gas and ash. Dark finger-like splotches show recent lava flows. The bright white areas are clouds.

Satellite Remote Sensing

Satellites orbiting high above the earth can gather surprisingly detailed information about volcanoes below. Before an eruption, satellites can detect . . .

- changes in the shape of the volcano, such as swelling or depressions formed from the movement of magma underground

- hot spots (areas of higher surface temperatures) on the volcano, suggesting vents or fumaroles are heating up or that hot magma has pooled just beneath the surface

- sulfur dioxide emissions from a volcano, which suggests magma is rising toward the surface

During and after an eruption, the satellites can track . . .

- the location of lava flows, mudflows, and other eruption materials

- lava domes growing on a volcano

- the shape, texture, temperature, location, and movement of ash clouds and columns, which can destroy airplanes' engines

- the amount of volcanic gases erupted, which can help scientists estimate the size of the eruption

Indonesian volcanologists monitor earthquakes on Mount Merapi from Yogyakarta.

* * * * *

On October 25, Merapi begins pumping out huge amounts of volcanic gases. It's time get people out of harm's way, Surono decides.

He grabs the transmitter on the radio and pushes the transmit button: LEVEL FOUR, LEVEL FOUR. WE HAVE MOVED TO LEVEL FOUR.

Radios throughout the region relay the message: AWAS! AWAS! EVACUATE! EVACUATE!

Villagers hustle out of their houses, shouting to their neighbors: EVACUATE! EVACUATE!

Villagers flock to shelters outside the evacuation zone. A five-bedroom house at one center is crammed with

"The magnitude of the energy released by the shaking and the magnitude of swelling was much greater than what they had seen before," John says. "Knowing Merapi's history, its potential for larger eruptions and larger pyroclastic flows, we were all better prepared to say this isn't going to be just another small eruption. It's going to be something much bigger."

John and Surono agree that the old maps marking hazard zones are no good. The last eruption had changed the shape of the summit. And the eruption could be much bigger. Blasts and pyroclastic flows could run farther south toward population centers, or anywhere, really.

There's no time to draw a new hazard map, so they discuss something simpler. On a map, Surono draws a series of evacuation zone rings around the summit, five, ten, fifteen, and twenty kilometers (3, 6, 9, and 12 miles) out. That will have to do.

nearly one hundred people. Evacuation centers overflow, and people move on to the next nearest shelter.

More than 20,000 people living within 6.2 miles (10 kilometers) of the summit evacuate. Many people, such as Ponco Sumarto, a sixty-five-year-old grandmother, trek all the way to a tent camp ten miles (16 kilometers) from the volcano. "I just have to follow orders to take shelter here for safety even though I'd rather like to stay at home," she says. Her grown children and many other villagers stay behind to take care of livestock and crops.

But many follow the lead of Mbah Maridjan, a spiritual leader and medicine man, known as the "guardian" of Mount Merapi, who refuses to leave the volcano. Some villagers believe he knows they will be safe and also refuse to evacuate.

Ismail's family, who live less than a mile (2 kilometers) away from

Thousands of people were evacuated to temporary tent camps when Mount Merapi threatened to blow.

This evacuation map displayed in the town of Magelang high on Mount Merapi's flanks shows locals the location and amenities at the closest evacuation centers.

the observatory in the village of Krinjing, leave behind their one cow, five chickens, and a field lush with red chili peppers, green beans, tomatoes, corn, and long beans. Ismail stays behind to take care of the farm and observe.

To Ismail, Mount Merapi feels like a loaded gun pointed right at him.

Thirty-five hours later, it happens. On October 26, in the late afternoon, seismographs in observatories around the volcano begin whining— *EEE EEE EEE. WOO WOO WOO!* The volcano quakes violently.

At Babadan, Ismail's radio screams. It's Surono radioing from Yogyakarta. GO, GO, GO NOW! POST EMPTY NOW! NOW! NOW!

The volcano explodes, blasting hot ash 7.5 miles (12 kilometers) into the air and sending an avalanche of hot rocks and gases pouring into the mountain villages.

Ismail jumps on his motorcycle and rides through the village, yelling, EVACUATE! EVACUATE! as white ash rains down from the sky, coating everything.

People who defied the evacuation orders flee down the mountain, driving, biking, and running to the nearest refugee camp 2.5 miles (4 kilometers) away, with no more than the clothes on their backs.

Slamet Riady, sixty-four, has survived many Merapi eruptions. "This was bigger than the past eruptions," he says. "They rang the sirens, and we had no time to bring anything. The most important thing was to save ourselves."

Ash covers the city of Yogyakarta like a film. Not everyone escapes; more than thirty people die. Mbah Maridjan's charred body is found in the ruins of his home, bowed down in a position of prayer.

Mount Merapi erupts.

Residents ride their motorcycles in Yogyakarta, blanketed by volcanic ash falling from Mount Merapi's eruption.

Singing Seismograph

When they were first developed in the late 1800s, seismographs recorded earthquakes with a needle that scratched special paper or an instrument called a smoked drum. The only sound was a *scratch, scratch.*

Today when a volcano quakes, the ground shaking moves a magnet within a wire coil in the seismometer. The movement generates voltage (electricity).

The seismometer amplifies the signals and translates them into tones, which can be transmitted to the observatory (or anywhere via the Internet). The tones are converted into the wavy lines on the seismograph but can also be heard as wavering tones on the radio. Observers often carry radios so they can hear when a volcano is singing a warning.

Merapi observer Ismail radios Yogyakarta from Babadan
Observatory during a rare clear view of the volcano.

CHAPTER SEVEN

Mount Merapi's Next Move

This Synthetic Aperture Radar (SAR) satellite image of Mount Merapi taken on October 26, 2010, shows how the eruption removed a lava dome and enlarged and deepened the summit crater.

When the sun rises, clouds completely obscure Mount Merapi. The Indonesian scientists can't see what happened to the summit during the eruption.

When John and his USGS colleagues check satellite images, they're surprised. "The eruption didn't form a dome as we expected. It was an explosive event that blew out part of the old dome complex and made an entirely new crater at the summit. That immediately changed the scenario. We were definitely seeing something we haven't seen before, something much more like what happens before the big explosive eruptions."

The radar data Julie collects also shows Surono where the pyroclastic flows went. They reached five miles (8 kilometers) down the flanks of the volcano, just a mile (2 kilometers) short of the evacuation line. "That's a little too close for comfort, but the evacuation worked," John says. "They saved a lot of lives in that first eruption. But we don't know if Merapi's done."

Ismail at Babadan and Purwono, another observer at another high-up observatory, are glad their families had been evacuated. But they return to their posts to watch the volcano.

John wants to get Surono a better picture of what's going on at the cloud- and ash-cloaked volcano. That takes invoking the International Charter for Space and Natural Disasters.

Farm animals are many Indonesian villagers' most prized possessions.

Surono, head of the Center for Volcanology and Geologic Hazard Mitigation (CVGHM), part of the Geological Agency in Indonesia, speaks at a news conference about Mount Merapi.

The charter asks nations around the world to share information from satellites on an area of concern, in this case Mount Merapi. Invoking the charter gives VDAP and the Indonesians access to images of the volcano from Germany, Canada, Japan, Italy, and other nations.

"These images became the only way of really being able to assess what's happening at the volcano," says John. "Knowing the situation at the summit is critical, because collapse of the summit and pyroclastic flows are the biggest dangers to people's lives in the villages."

Photos and data of the volcano pour into USGS offices in Alaska, Virginia, and are sent on to Vancouver, Washington. John and Julie analyze the results and pass their analyses immediately to Surono.

"No additional changes detected at the summit."

The next three days, Mount Merapi is quiet.

"There was certainly a reduction in activity," Surono tells the press. "I don't know if Merapi is going to stop. It's too early to say."

Except for the volcano observers, people are prohibited from returning to the evacuation zone. But many trudge and scooter back to their homes and farms to grab valuables and feed their livestock. Cows are rural Indonesia's most prized possessions, and families' most valuable assets.

On October 30, Merapi sends off another warning: a small but explosive eruption. Traffic in Yogyakarta grinds to a standstill as motorists stop to gape at a gray plume of ash and superheated gas that shoots into the sky and tumbles down the flanks.

People who snuck into the evacuation zone hustle out again. "I was so scared," says a villager named Natya. "I heard this loud sound from the volcano. We were told to get on a police truck. I was panicking."

A villager from Kaliurang had returned to the village to feed his animals when he heard police sirens and neighbors screaming. "He only had his boxer shorts on," his wife, Bu Suharno, says. "He had to race back down the mountain on his motorbike in his underwear."

This SAR satellite image of Mount Merapi taken on November 4, 2010, shows the dome growing on the summit.

As Mount Merapi ramped up, government officials opened more evacuation centers farther from the volcano.

* * * * *

The scientists in the United States and in Yogyakarta and the observers on the mountain wait for Mount Merapi to make its next move. Maybe it will start building a lava dome. And if it does, maybe it will peacefully build for a while and then slip back into dormancy. "We're still very concerned that Merapi could send off more explosions, but still we tended to expect a dome extrusion and tapering off," says John.

Then a radar photo of the summit from the German space agency flashes on John's computer: a dome appears—a massive, fast-growing monster.

Text messages fly across the globe.

"New lava dome started."

"Lava dome growing very rapidly."

"Lava dome growing VERY rapidly."

"Our remote sensing teams were working around the clock," says John. "We'd give estimates of the rate of the growth of the lava dome and those were extraordinarily rapid rates, more rapid than they'd ever seen before."

Tension ramps up in Indonesia and halfway across the world in Vancouver. "Communicating directly with Surono and relaying all of this data, it's almost like we're there," says John. "It's gotten to that point, with international communications as good as they are, that you start feeling personally responsible for what you're seeing and communicating long distance, and for how your interpretations are affecting people's lives thousands of miles away."

The scientists all start fearing the worst. On November 3, Surono and government officials evacuate people to fifteen kilometers (9.3 miles) and begin setting up evacuation camps even farther from the volcano.

November 5, 2010

BRRRRING! Another early-morning phone call jars John awake. It's nighttime at Merapi. The volcano is shaking violently, destroying seismometers all over its flanks. The only one still working records so many big earthquakes that the seismograph is a continuous black blob, with the needle swinging rail to rail. To be shaking that hard, this eruption has to be huge.

But it's pitch black and cloudy. The Indonesian volcanologists can't see a thing. "I'm thinking of moving the evacuation level out to twenty kilometers," Surono says. "John, what do you think?"

That would mean evacuating roughly 30,000 more villagers who live within twenty kilometers (12 miles) of the summit. All those people would have to leave their homes, their farms, and their livelihoods. And tens of thousands of people who had already been evacuated to camps at fifteen kilometers (9 miles) would have to move again.

But with the troubling satellite images and now the violent shaking, John's response is immediate. "Yes, I agree—do it."

Lightning strikes as Mount Merapi erupts, as seen from Ketep village in Indonesia's Central Java province, Magelang.

Searing pyroclastic flows roar down Merapi's flank as it erupts.

Merapi observer Purwono has hidden in this underground bunker during other Merapi eruptions. "If I had been in here during this eruption, I would have cooked like a chicken in an oven," he says.

Surono and his colleagues immediately radio the observatories and villages all around the volcano. MOVE PEOPLE OUT! MOVE THEM OUT PAST TWENTY KILOMETERS!

Across the broad flanks of Merapi, government officials, observers, and other villagers literally wake up their neighbors and tell them to run down the hill.

Mosques with speakers ring out: ERUPSI! ERUPSI! AWAS! AWAS! People grab sticks and start whacking the kentongans, huge pieces of thick bamboo cut open on one side used to call people to prayer—or to call for an evacuation.

Men, women, and children stream down the mountain, on foot, on motorbike, piled in trucks and buses. Ismail quickly fills his cow's water trough and shovels in as much grass and grain as will fit, closes the barn door, and hurries to an evacuation camp.

Soon after, Mount Merapi blows.

With a roar, it hurls an ash cloud 55,000 feet (16,764 meters) into the air. Ash and rocks pellet from the sky.

To save his life, observer Purwono grabs his motorbike and speeds down the mountain. It's raining and the rain mixes with ash, blinding him and making his bike slip and skid.

A village on the flanks of Mount Merapi before and after the devastating eruption of 2010.

Most of the village had already evacuated, so Purwono picks up speed going downhill, the growling volcano at his back. He rounds a curve, his wheels skid out from under him, and he falls hard, slamming his shoulder on the pavement. Dark, sooty rain pelts down. He has no choice but to pick himself and his motorcycle up and race down the shaking, exploding volcano.

Ash, rocks, boulders, and hot gases that shoot out from the summit also begin rolling down the volcano, picking up speed as gravity pulls them down slope. The summit collapses and a searing hot pyroclastic flow—as hot as 1,100 degrees Fahrenheit (600 degrees Celsius)—surges down the mountain, roaring like a runaway train.

The superheated gases and rocks plow over villages on the flanks. They roil through the fields, singeing trees, crops, and livestock, melting satellite dishes, blasting out windows, and turning doors and fence posts to tinder.

The pyroclastic flows spread more than fifteen kilometers (9 miles) from the summit, smothering entire villages, blowing down trees and houses, and burning everything in their paths. The vegetation is stripped bare. Everything's charred. Nothing survives the pyroclastic flows and surges.

The ash cloud rises over Yogyakarta and drifts south. Air thickens with gray ash. Thousands of ash-covered people holding handkerchiefs to their mouths bolt for safety. Evacuees huddle in stadiums, government buildings, schools, and tent camps. More than 300,000 people are displaced.

It's a massive eruption, a catastrophe, a tragedy. More than three hundred people die.

In the tragedy of those deaths, the media and the rest of the world miss something.

The success of the prediction and evacuation is astounding.

More than 2,600 houses on the flanks were either completely destroyed or heavily damaged. The 10,000 to 20,000 people who lived in those houses, who worked up in those fields, were saved by the evacuations.

They're safe—for now.

"We know two very frightening things about volcanoes like Mount Merapi," John says. "People always move back into harm's way . . . and the volcano always erupts again."

John has another worry. He knows that Merapi is capable of even bigger eruptions—and that sometimes big eruptions happen in clusters. This eruption, terrifying as it was, could just be a hint of what is yet to come.

Refugees at a temporary evacuation center in Yogyakarta, Indonesia, following the climactic eruption of Mount Merapi on November 5, 2010. Tens of thousands of lives were saved by the timely evacuations.

Residents evacuate a danger zone as Mount Merapi erupts ash and launches pyroclastic flows near Balerante village.

Rainwater after Mount Merapi's eruption created massive mudflows, or lahars, that swept down the Putih River, destroying villages along the banks.

CHAPTER EIGHT

The Mystery of the Missing Ash

Pak Nur Cholis in his lahar-damaged house.

Five months after the eruption and evacuation at Mount Merapi, three VDAP volcanologists, John Pallister, Julie Griswold, and Angie Diefenbach, along with seven Indonesian scientists, meet at a hotel in Yogyakarta and climb into three minivans. Each is stocked with a full case of bottled water. Though it's only 8 a.m., the sun is already blazing, and heat squiggles rise from the road.

Mount Merapi is shrouded by clouds. But not far from downtown, the destruction wrought by the eruption is obvious. A mudflow from the eruption swept down the Putih River and wiped out houses and businesses along the highway not far from the city. Some shells of houses remain, filled almost to the ceiling with gray mud.

The villagers have just begun digging out. They have managed shoulder-high paths to their doors. They have packed down a narrow trail for motorcycles to travel on. They have planted crops, already, in the gray ashy sand. One house already has a new red-shingled roof.

Pak Nur Cholis, skin glistening with sweat, shovels ash and sand out of his living

Workers harvest tons of volcanic ash and rocks from Mount Merapi's eruption to make cement and other building materials.

room. "I think it will take three to four years, but we can move back," he says. "The government is building a dam to protect us." He smiles. "In the meantime, I make one hundred thousand rupiah for each truckload of ash." That's about thirteen dollars per truckload. "Merapi can be dangerous," he says. "But it is also a blessing."

Everywhere Merapi has laid down ash, backhoes dig and scoop. Huge dump trucks heaped with gray sand back out onto the highway for delivery to construction companies. Women strap toaster-size lava blocks to their backs to sell to builders or to use themselves.

"Human erosion," Julie quips. "It's amazing how quickly people have mobilized and moved huge masses of volcanic debris."

But the Indonesian and VDAP volcanologists are more interested in ash fall that has *not* been moved. They begin to search for a spot where ash from the eruption has not been disturbed.

The vans pull over. The scientists slide out of the cars, climb over a pile of garbage, and work their way around a cement building to a small overgrown lot.

Forty steps from the buzzing highway, Angie raises her hand shovel to the sky and brings it down. *CHOP*. Again. *CHOP*. Angie's wearing jeans, hiking boots, and a safari-type shirt. She and everyone else are already sweating minutes from leaving the air-conditioned vans.

Angie pulls back a clump of grass and everyone crowds around. There, under the shallow grass roots, is a clear strip of gray ash.

With great rustling and muttering, everyone pulls out notebooks and pencils, tape measures, Global Positioning Systems (GPS), and cameras.

Angie digs a neat cross-section. Everyone can see clearly now the layers of brown soil and gray ash.

Don't Forget the Toilet Paper

VDAP scientists working in the field carry backpacks filled with essential tools and supplies. They pack . . .

shovel for digging

knife for scraping

plastic bags for samples

permanent marker for marking samples

tape measure to estimate depths

gardening trowel (to smooth soil to see ash layers clearly)

toilet paper (local toilets may not have it)

diarrhea medicine (this common malady of international travel can hit anytime)

field notebook

pens or pencils

hat

sunglasses

GPS to mark exact coordinates

map

first-aid kit

water

camera

compass

rain jacket (it can pour anytime)

passport/ID and money

snacks (scientists bring breakfast bars, candy, even sardines for quick energy)

Julie Griswold (left) takes ash measurements and samples with Indonesian volcanologists Supriyati Andreastuti (center) and Anjar Heriwaseso.

Indonesian volcanolgists Supriyati Andreastuti (left) and Dewi Sri Sayudi (center) discuss an ash sample with John Pallister.

"I'll scrape it," offers Supriyati Andreastuti, an Indonesian volcanologist and an expert on Merapi's past eruptions. Supriyati is a compact woman with thick curly hair, bright brown eyes, and a warm smile. She takes a gardening trowel and smooths the surface.

Julie drops to her knee and sticks the end of a tape measure at the bottom of the hole.

"Five centimeters," Supriyati says.

"Four point five," Julie suggests.

"Let's try another spot," John says.

The group disperses into small clusters, where the process happens again. Someone digs. Someone smooths. Someone measures. They all jot notes in their field notebooks. They all take photos of the layered cross-section of soil and ash. And they all check their GPS and mark the exact coordinates of their location.

Why would ten volcanologists hack through grass to uncover a mere five centimeters (about 2 inches) of ash in an abandoned lot ten miles (16 kilometers) from a volcano?

"To figure out what Mount Merapi might do next, we need to know exactly what the volcano did already," John explains. "Based on the amount of gas the Indonesians and the satellites measured coming from Merapi during the eruption, we made initial estimates of the amount of ash and other debris erupted," John says. "But it looks like our estimate was off—way off." He pauses. "And that could be very worrisome."

If huge amounts of gas came out without the corresponding amount of ash and lava, then where did all that gas come from? The most likely possibility is also the scariest: The gas may have come from a new batch of magma deep inside the earth. There may be a pool of

Angie and John dig a hole in a soccer field to measure the ash layer beneath the grass.

new magma underground, waiting to come up. Mount Merapi may be just warming up.

The scientists kneel beside the hole, pinch the ash, and smoosh it around in their hands. They jot more notes.

John and Supriyati confer. "See the ash at the base, the pink," Supriyati says. "That is maybe from October twenty-sixth."

They take a pinch of whiter ash just above the thin line of pink. "This has finer grains," John observes.

Supriyati nods.

"And the gray?" That is by far the thickest layer, making up most of the five centimeters.

"The fifth of November." Everyone nods, remembering that day, the shaking, the rumbling, the huge dark ash cloud.

"Think about what people were living through when this happened," John whispers.

He clears his throat. "It rained that day, right?" John asks.

"Yes, after three p.m. all through that day and the next." Supriyati wipes sweat from her brow.

"Maybe the rain did some mixing." They all nod. That would explain some of the variation in the ash layers that they find.

"We should take a sample," someone suggests.

Supriyati carves out what looks like a small square ash cake. Then she slips the trowel under most of the cake and puts it into a small plastic bag. She carves off the next layer and the pink layer and slips them into bags, too, so they can study them back in the labs.

As they head back to the vans, John asks: "So how far from the volcano did ash fall?"

"At eighteen kilometers from the summit, it is only three centimeters deep," says Dewi Sri Sayudi. One of the senior volcanologists in Yogyakarta, Dewi wears the traditional Muslim headscarf worn by almost half of the women in the region. To keep off the sun, it's topped with a conical straw hat often worn by rice farmers.

"But how far before it turned to nothing?" John wants to know.

"So far, we have only looked close in," Dewi says.

"So that is the question," says John.

"That is the question," Supriyati agrees.

To answer that question, the Indonesian and VDAP scientists work side by side in the field—in soccer fields, that is. Soccer fields are perfect places to measure ash depth. They are flat and open, so the ash fall lands in a smooth, uniform layer. They are far enough off the road for the ash not to be disturbed by turbulence from passing traffic.

So all day, the scientists chop small holes at the edges of soccer fields—soccer fields near rice paddies, near papaya plantations, near banana and coconut groves, next to houses, schools, and stores, near lines of laundry baking in the hot sun.

Indonesian volcanologist Dewi Sri Sayudi studies a lava rock with a magnifying glass.

Sometimes the scientists can make out the layer of pink ash, sometimes not. Sometimes the ash is thicker than they expect, sometimes thinner.

Villagers abandon their brooms, their shovels, and their crops to find out why this odd group of people is studying small holes they dig at the edges of soccer fields.

Supriyati and Dewi greet them all warmly and ask in Indonesian or the local language, Javanese, what they remember from the eruption. One woman in a bright skirt and headscarf tells how her daughter gave birth to a son as the volcano erupted. How the rain fell, the ash fell.

"How much ash?" Supriyati asks.

A cluster of women hold up four fingers, signifying four centimeters (1.6 inches).

Near a farm, a man holding a papaya holds out three fingers (1.2 inches).

Kids riding bikes around a soccer field hold out two fingers (0.8 inches).

In a forested area farther out, a toothless woman in a frayed peach dress and flip-flops comes out of her house to ask what the group is doing.

Supriyati meets her with a big smile and an outstretched hand. The scientist asks the woman if she remembers the eruption. The woman nods yes. "Did ash fall here?" The woman shakes her head no.

Nearby, the scientists dig and dig and can find no ash. They have found the edge. The ash fall ceased much closer to the volcano's summit than they had expected. Not a good thing.

VDAP and Indonesian volcanologists have found that gardening trowels make great tools for smoothing ash layers.

Indonesian volcanologist Dewi Sri Sayudi (right) interviews villagers about the amount of ash that fell during Mount Merapi's eruption.

CHAPTER NINE

What Happened Here?

Houses in the village of **P**etung on the flanks of Mount Merapi were completely destroyed from the blast, pyroclastic flows and surges, and mudflows.

From their day in the field, the volcanologists have a decent estimate of how much ash blew out from the volcano into the sky. It's about half of what they expected to find. But how much surged down the flanks? Knowing that will help them calculate the total amount of material erupted.

To find out, the Indonesian scientists lead the VDAP scientists from the city and toward the summit, to Dusun Petung, a village obliterated by the eruption.

On the highway, the surroundings slowly change from a gritty urban landscape to a green, lush patchwork of rice paddies. As the bumpy road begins to climb up the flanks of Merapi, the land becomes

John Pallister closely studies the windowsill of a house to figure out what eruptive forces destroyed the village.

terraced with neat rectangular fields of tomatoes, cauliflower, and a popular vegetable called cassava. Soon the fields turn gray with ash, but crops planted since the eruption thrive.

When the caravan reaches Dusun Petung, the scientists park on the ash and climb over the piles of rubble and around the devastated houses. What exactly destroyed the village? A pyroclastic flow and surge, a lahar, or both?

Supriyati pokes at some debris with her toe. It's soft and crumbly. She taps her foot on it and then her shovel. THUD, THUD. It's loose and soft. "Pyroclastic flow," she says.

John picks up crumbled bits of glass from a windowsill. "Yes, a quick pulse from the surge," he adds. "The force and the heat shattered the glass." He scrapes his fingernail along the charred wood of the windowpane. "The wood is singed but not burned through, so the heat surge must have been quick but intense."

Supriyati points out the columns of a porch that lie flattened on a concrete slab. They all fell the same way, literally pointing in the direction of the blast. "When I see this I go back to Mount St. Helens in my mind," she says. She had visited VDAP offices at the USGS Cascades Volcano Observatory for training in 2003. "I was not used to such big blasts," she says. "It really helps me understand better what happened here."

"That melding of local expertise, extensive experience with eruptions and evacuations, and international collaboration has made Indonesian volcanologists some of the best in the world at dealing with volcano crises," John says.

After poking around and finding areas of hard, compacted, cementlike soil, the scientists agree that the village was hit by a triple whammy of pyroclastic flows, pyroclastic surges, and a mudflow. But how much new magma came out?

The scientists fan out, dig holes, and measure. What they see makes them pause, scratch their heads, and mop their brows worriedly. The deposit is only ten inches (25 centimeters) deep. They would have

American and Indonesian volcanologists observe how the fallen rails from a porch of a destroyed building point in the direction of the blast.

expected three feet (one meter) or more. And a lot of it looks like old material that just got moved by the power of the blast.

The Indonesians take the VDAP team closer to the steaming summit, to an area that was once the village of Gendol. Now it is no more than tire tracks on a thick ash deposit and makeshift huts offering snacks and photos to rubbernecking tourists. The entrance is marked by a burned-out scooter.

Off in the distance, the jagged crater looks like a huge jaw gaping open to this side of the mountain. A deep, scarred canyon leads from the crater mouth far down toward Yogyakarta. The scientists gaze across the gray plain, past the scarred canyon, to the strangely green flank on the other side, where three villages remain intact.

"This really drives home how hard it is to predict exactly where the pyroclastic flows and their surges will go . . ." John says.

"Look," Dewi says. "People have moved back."

After the village of Gendol was completely destroyed by Mount Merapi's eruption, locals built makeshift huts on the piles of ash and lava to sell photos and snacks to curious visitors.

Indeed, the villages look alive, inhabited.

John turns to her, startled. "I thought the government was going to bar people from living this high up."

Dewi shakes her head soberly. "Once people have moved back, it will be very hard to relocate them."

The scientists are grim as they walk toward the edge of the cliff of the gaping canyon.

"Can we get down there?" John asks.

The drop is sheer and steep, so the question is preposterous. Everyone laughs, relieving some of the tension, some of the worry.

John wants to go into the canyon so he can get an elevation reading from his GPS. With that, he can compare the post-eruption elevation with the elevation level before the eruption. The difference is the depth of the deposit.

"I could throw my GPS down there," Julie jokes.

"It would be nice to have a photograph of this area before the eruption," says John.

"I have one," Dewi says.

All eyes turn to Dewi.

"What was the shape of the valley before the eruption?" John asks.

"Steep on both sides and flat at the bottom," she says. "I think the deposit is twenty to twenty-five meters thick here."

The Americans are surprised at how quickly Dewi makes her estimate. She flips to a clean page of a notebook to explain. "I know the dimensions of the canyon before the eruption," she says. She starts drawing and calculating, showing how big the canyon was before, how much shallower it is now.

Julie watches over her shoulder. Her eyes widen.

"It's half full. The flow filled the canyon halfway up," she realizes.

Dewi nods and puts her pencil down.

Scientists (from left to right) Angie, Supriyati, John, and Dewi gaze at the eruption deposit left in a canyon high on Mount Merapi's flank.

They both gaze across the canyon to the red roofs of the houses on the other side—the villages untouched by the pyroclastic flows.

"If you're right," Julie says, and her eyes suggest she thinks Dewi is right, "it's very frightening. This flow had an empty canyon to roll down and still some overflow destroyed the villages on this side. If there is another eruption as big or bigger with the canyon already half filled up . . ."

She pauses and takes a deep breath. "If there is another big eruption, debris will completely fill the canyon and the flow will launch out on both sides." She spreads her arms, indicating the whole flank.

Dewi nods.

"Oh, these poor people," Julie says, looking across at the peaceful villages. "Those villages will be gone next time. They will be gone. I hope the people understand that."

For some reason, Dewi doesn't seem as upset. She has worked in the shadow of this volcano for many years and has seen many things. "Four years after the 2006 eruption, the entire deposit was cleaned out of the canyon," she says.

Julie doesn't follow at first. "What?"

"The rain washed it all away."

"So this will all be washed away," Julie says, more a statement than a question.

"If there is enough time before the next big eruption," says Dewi, "the canyon might be cleaned out and those villages might survive after all."

That's good news—and bad. Heavy rain on the volcano may sweep away the ash and rocks in that deep deposit. But that leaves villages downstream vulnerable to dangerous mudflows of volcanic debris. That's why Dewi, Supriyati, Ismail, and all the other volcanologists and observers on Merapi will keep a close and constant eye on this volcano.

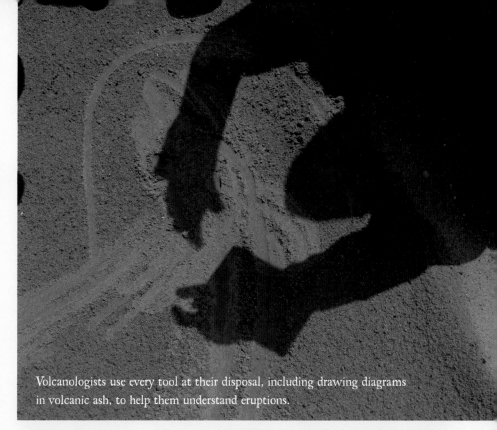

Volcanologists use every tool at their disposal, including drawing diagrams in volcanic ash, to help them understand eruptions.

A melted **TV** remote from a home in Gendol is testament to the heat of the eruption that destroyed the village.

The steep road up to Babadan Observatory.

CHAPTER TEN

Living and Working in the Shadow of a Volcano

Volcano observer Ismail outside Babadan Observatory, where he lives and works under the shadow of Mount Merapi.

Four days after Mount Merapi's massive eruption, Ismail rode his motorbike up to the village of Krinjing just six kilometers (3.7 miles) from the summit to check on his house, his crops, and his animals. More than ten centimeters (4 inches) of ash blanketed his village, but the pyroclastic flow missed it. His family's house was coated with ash, but still standing.

Ismail went around back to the small barn. Their cow was very thin and hungry. All five chickens had died. Their food had been covered in ash. They must have starved.

Villagers who live on the flanks of Mount Merapi cherish the volcano—
and their farm animals.

A month later he, his family, and most of the other people in the
village moved back.

Ismail has been even more vigilant since he took up his post again
at the Babadan Observatory. He's gotten a glimpse of what this volcano
can do. "I am afraid of another big eruption," he says. "I know Merapi
will erupt again."

But he also knows that he and his family would move back again.

To Ismail and the other people who live on its flanks, Mount
Merapi is not just a danger. It's a valuable resource. Ash and mud from
mudflows make cement for their roads, bridges, and buildings. Lava
blocks are the building blocks of their homes. Ash fertilizes the fields
that feed them.

Thousands of crop terraces form shallow steps all the way up
the mountain as if the volcano were a temple, and to many villagers,
Merapi is a temple. They cannot abandon it. They can pray, plow, and
carry their harvest to market. They can leave at a moment's notice—
and return and rebuild. That is life on Merapi.

Without scientists watching their backs, many, many more people
would be killed when Merapi erupts, that much is clear. But if more
people died, would fewer people move back? Would fewer people take
the risk of living in the shadow of a dangerous volcano?

Maybe. For a while. But the volcano gives the people everything
they need: food, cool air, building materials, and beauty.

The villagers trust they will be taken care of—if not by the
volcano itself, then by the scientists who watch it, study it, and try to
understand it. Scientists whose numbers and skills are growing, thanks
to VDAP.

"Pinatubo and Merapi are dramatic examples where VDAP's ef-
forts helped saved tens of thousands of lives," says John. "I'm so proud
of our role in that. But I really think the capacity-building we're doing
around the world will have an even more lasting impact than crisis
response. It's the volcanologists on location on the ground having the
know-how and tools they need to read dangerous volcanoes that will
ultimately result in the most saved lives."

VDAP is a brave team of scientists trying to keep millions of
people around the globe safe. It's difficult—almost impossible—work.

"Thank goodness," John says, "we don't have to do it alone."

VDAP director John Pallister studies the devastation from Mount Merapi's eruption.

Volcanic Vocabulary

ACTIVE: An active volcano is one that has erupted in the last 10,000 years.

ASH: Tiny bits of volcanic rock, glass, and minerals.

ASH CLOUD: A mass of airborne ash and volcanic gas.

ASH FALL: Airborne volcanic ash from an eruption cloud or column that falls from the sky.

BLAST: A horizontally directed explosion of hot gas and ash from a volcano that can move at hundreds of miles an hour with enough force to blow down a forest.

CARBON DIOXIDE (CO_2): An invisible, odorless volcanic gas. Except for water vapor, it is the most abundant gas that comes out of volcanoes.

CONDUIT: A pipelike passageway through which magma rises to the surface.

COSPEC (CORRELATION SPECTROMETER): An instrument that measures the gas sulfur dioxide, now mainly replaced by smaller digital differential optical absorption spectrometer (DOAS) instruments.

CORE: The very hot region in the center of the earth composed mainly of iron and nickel.

CRATER: A bowl formed by either a volcanic explosion or the collapse of a volcano.

CRATER FLOOR: The bottom of a crater.

CRATER WALL: The sides of a crater.

CRUST: The earth's outermost layer.

DOME: A mound or pile of thick lava that can grow very large and steep and can collapse to produce pyroclastic flows.

DORMANT: Not having erupted for a long time but capable of erupting in the future.

EARTHQUAKE SWARM: A group of earthquakes happening in the same place, one after another and in rapid succession.

ERUPTION: When magma from under a volcano reaches the earth's surface.

EVACUATION ZONE: A marked area where most or all people are ordered to leave temporarily.

EXPLOSIVE ERUPTION: An eruption in which magma, ash, and gases blast out of a volcano with great force.

FISSURE: A crack in a volcano, sometimes marking a fault zone where a volcano is being pulled apart.

FLANK: The side of a volcano.

FUMAROLE: A crack in a volcano's surface where gases and ash can escape.

GEOLOGIST: A scientist who studies the earth.

GPS (GLOBAL POSITIONING SYSTEM): A radio receiver that can pinpoint an exact location using satellite signals.

HARMONIC TREMOR: Continuous, rhythmic earthquakes that can happen before or during volcanic eruptions.

HAZARD: A danger or risk of harm; also the event that causes risk, such as a mudflow.

HAZARD ASSESSMENT: An evaluation of the areas that may be affected by volcanic activity during or after an eruption.

HAZARD MAP: A map that shows the areas around a volcano that might be affected by an eruption.

HOT SPOT: An area on the surface of a volcano where the temperature is higher than its surroundings. Hot spots usually indicate that magma is near the surface. Also a geologic term for places in the interior of plates where upswelling of the earth's mantle creates volcanoes.

HYDROGEN SULFIDE (H_2S): A gas with a rotten-egg smell. A volcano may emit hydrogen sulfide when the volcanic gas sulfur dioxide mixes with water.

LAHAR: The Indonesian name for a volcanic mudflow, a term used by volcanologists worldwide.

LANDSLIDE: A large mass of earth falling or sliding rapidly under the force of gravity.

LAVA: Magma that has erupted to the surface.

LAVA BOMB: Erupted lava chunks larger than 2½ inches (64 milimeters) in diameter.

LAVA FLOW: An outpouring of molten lava from a volcano.

MAGMA: Molten rock that is still underground, typically containing melted and partially melted rock, mineral crystals, and dissolved gases.

MAGMA CHAMBER: An area of melted or partially melted rock and gases beneath a volcano.

MAGNITUDE: A number that represents the power of an earthquake. Each increase in number (such as from 1 to 2) represents a tenfold increase in power.

MANTLE: The soft, hot part of the inside of the earth between the core and the crust.

MONITORING STATION: A spot where scientists have placed equipment such as seismographs to gather information about a volcano.

MUDFLOW: A thick mixture of water, ash, and volcanic rock that is pulled downhill by gravity. A mudflow is also known by the Indonesian term lahar.

OBSERVATORY: A place where geologists gather, house equipment, and study data. Volcano observatories often have a direct view of a volcano.

PLATES: Massive slabs of the earth's crust. Many volcanoes occur around the edges of plates.

PLUG: Hardened lava that closes a vent.

PLUME: A cloud of water vapor, volcanic gases, and/or volcanic ash that can rise from a volcanic vent.

PUMICE: A light-colored (gray or whitish) volcanic rock so filled with gas bubbles that it may float on water.

PYROCLASTIC FLOW: Hot volcanic gases and ash clouds that can race down the flanks of an erupting volcano with tremendous speed and destructive force and heat.

SEISMOGRAM: A record produced by a seismograph (or seismometer).

SEISMOGRAPH (ALSO SEISMOMETER):
A tool that measures and records ground vibrations, especially from earthquakes.

STEAM ERUPTION: A blast of gas from a volcano that may or may not include some ash.

STEAM PLUME: A mass of steam and ash coming from a volcano.

STRATOSPHERE: A region of the upper atmosphere extending from about six miles (10 kilometers) to about thirty miles (50 kilometers) above the earth.

SULFUR DIOXIDE (SO$_2$): A volcanic gas.

SUMMIT: The top of a volcano.

SURGE: A horizontally directed gush of hot ash and gas similar to a blast but typically coming from the front and sides of a pyroclastic flow.

TREMOR: Many earthquakes; ground-shaking.

VDAP (THE VOLCANO DISASTER ASSISTANCE PROGRAM): A partnership between the U.S. Agency for International Development's Office of Foreign Disaster Assistance and the U.S. Geological Survey, which has a mission to prevent international volcano crises from becoming disasters.

VENT: An opening in a volcano at the surface through which lava, ash, and gas can erupt.

VOLCANO CRISIS: The period when a volcano has become active and may be heading toward an eruption that could endanger people or property, as well as the period of continued or diminishing activity following an eruption in which there is still a danger.

VOLCANIC DEBRIS: Ash, lava, pumice, and other materials released from a volcano.

VOLCANIC HAZARD ZONE: An area around a volcano where property or people are likely to be harmed by volcanic activity or a volcanic eruption.

VOLCANOLOGIST: A scientist who studies volcanoes.

Our Deepest Appreciation

We want to thank the scientists of the Volcano Disaster Assistance Program for risking their lives to save others—and for making this book possible. The VDAP scientists allowed us to tag along in training sessions in their offices at the USGS Cascades Volcano Observatory and at Mount St. Helens and while on location at Mount Merapi in Indonesia. They found time between volcano crises to patiently and generously answer countless questions in many hours of interviews in person and by phone and to sift through old notes and photos to share with us.

We especially want to thank Andy Lockhart and John Pallister, Angie Diefenbach, John Ewert, Julie Griswold, Rowdy LeFevers, Wendy McCausland, and Marvin Couchman. Thank you too to the Chilean scientists Luis Enrique Franco and Gonzalo Andrés Hermosilla for sharing your experiences and thoughts with us. We also want to extend our warm thanks to the Indonesian scientists who so graciously hosted us during our trip to Mount Merapi—Dewi Sri Sayudi, Supriyati Andreastuti, Anjar Heriwaseso, Muhammad Nizar Firmansyah, Kusdaryanto, Radit Putra, Moch Muzani, and Pak Subandrio—as well as to local volcano observers Ismail and Purwono and to Armane Pandjenengan and Noer Cholik Asli for acting as our guides and translators. Your openness, kindness, knowledge, and laughter made the experience a joy and something we will remember forever. We hope this book honors your work and the work of all geologists worldwide who are dedicated to keeping people safe from the deadly power of volcanoes.

—Elizabeth Rusch and Tom Uhlman

The author would also like to thank Elizabeth (Tatty) Bartholomew and Erin Dees for their stellar research, editing, and transcribing skills, as well as the writers Addie Boswell, Nancy Coffelt, Ruth Feldman, Barbara Kerley, Amber Keyser, Michelle McCann, Sabina Rascol, Mary Rehmann, and Nicole Schrieber for their insightful comments and suggestions. Thanks to my editors Cynthia Platt and Erica Zappy and their team at Houghton Mifflin for all their wonderful work!

Chapter Notes

1. SLEEPING GIANT

"There came from this volcano . . ." Voight, p. 350.
"Ruiz activity is not dangerous." Voight, p. 357.
"Evacuate! Evacuate . . ." Scarth, p. 239.
"We were running . . ." Voight, p. 371.

2. NEVER AGAIN

"There was nothing anyone could do . . ." Lockhart interview.
"Volcanoes don't just erupt . . ." Lockhart interview.
"We'd be landing in . . ." Lockhart interview.
"Even in the best of situations . . ." Lockhart interview.
"Are we going to be heroes . . ." Belton, *Volcan's Deadly Warning*.
"Evacuations hold their own . . ." Lockhart interview.

3. MOUNT PINATUBO

"The ones that have been sleeping . . ." Thompson, p. 211.
"Hooooooly . . ." Thompson, p. 223.
"Get a little closer . . ." Lockhart interview.
"In the tall grass . . ." Lockhart interview.
"What is a pryoplastic?" to ". . . could be toast?" Thompson, p. 234.

4. TO EVACUATE OR NOT TO EVACUATE?

"Volcanoes don't necessarily move . . ." Lockhart interview.
"Geez, that's a lot . . ." to "Do it tomorrow." Lockhart interview.
"We were just incredibly . . ." Lockhart interview.
"I couldn't help . . ." Thompson, p. 268.
"Let's go!" to "Wahoo!" Lockhart interview.
"This is bad . . ." Lockhart interview.
"Should we evacuate?" Lockhart interview.
I could die... Lockhart interview.
"I figured that . . ." Lockhart interview.
"It was a huge . . ." Lockhart interview.
"We got it right . . ." Lockhart interview.

5. VOLCANO TRAINING CAMP

"Volcanoes don't wait . . ." Lockhart interview.
"When something is going on . . ." Lockhart interview.
"We try to make things . . ." Lockhart interview.
"You can bury this . . ." Lockhart interview.

"And with the humidity . . ." Franco interview.
"Any little critter . . ." Franco interview.
"I'm responsible . . ." Hermosilla interview.
"I want to see . . ." Hermosilla interview.
"You don't make that . . ." Lockhart interview.
"Before the eruption . . ." to "Nowhere is safe . . ." On-site observation by author.
"How long . . ." to "It's a pretty new way. . ." On-site observation by author.
"Yes, I want to understand . . ." Hermosilla interview.
"As more scientists get training . . ." Lockhart interview.
"Something is always . . ." Lockhart interview.
"The Ring of Fire keeps us . . ." Lockhart interview.
"We visited and got to know . . ." Pallister interview.
"So what's up . . ." Lockhart interview.
"We have increased . . ." Lockhart interview.
"The general feeling . . ." Pallister interview.

6. HOW DO YOU WATCH A VOLCANO YOU CAN'T SEE?

"I've already gone . . ." Pallister interview.
"Keep me posted . . ." Pallister interview.
"The smoke seemed . . ." to "Watch the volcano . . ." Ismail interview.
"Here's where we can . . ." Pallister interview.
"The magnitude . . ." Pallister interview.
"I just have to follow . . ." "Residents Evacuated."
"Go, go, go . . ." Ismail interview.
"This was bigger . . ." Quiano.

7. MOUNT MERAPI'S NEXT MOVE

"The eruption didn't form . . ." Pallister interview.
"That's a little too close . . ." Pallister interview.
"These images . . ." Pallister interview.
"No additional changes detected . . ." to "Still no change." Pallister interview.
"There was certainly a reduction . . ." Belford.
"I was so scared . . ." "New Volcanic Eruptions."
"He only had . . ." Belford and Carless.
"We're still very concerned . . ." Pallister interview.
"New lava dome . . ." to "Lava dome growing VERY . . ." Pallister interview.
"We'd give estimates . . ." Pallister interview.
"Communicating directly . . ." Pallister interview.
"I'm thinking of moving . . ." Pallister interview.
"Yes, do it." Pallister interview.
"We know two very frightening . . ." Pallister interview.

8. THE MYSTERY OF THE MISSING ASH

"I think it will take . . ." Cholis interview.
"Human erosion . . ." Griswold interview.
"I'll scrape it" to "Let's try another spot." On-site observation by the author.
"To figure out . . ." Pallister interview.
"See the ash at the base . . ." to "That is the question." On-site observation by the author.
"How much ash?" On-site observation by the author.

9. WHAT HAPPENED HERE?

"Pyroclastic flow" to "but the wood is singed . . ." On-site observation by the author.
"When I see this . . ." Andreastuti interview.
"That melding . . ." Pallister interview.
"This really drives home . . ." to "I think the deposit . . ." On-site observation by the author.
"I know the dimensions . . ." to "If there is enough time . . ." On-site observation by the author.

10. LIVING AND WORKING IN THE SHADOW OF A VOLCANO

"I am afraid . . ." Ismail interview.
"Pinatubo and Merapi . . ." Pallister interview.
"Thank goodness . . ." Pallister interview.
"We don't have frequent . . ." Lockhart interview.

Other facts and details not in quotation come from Scarth, Thompson, Bruce, and Voight; USGS fact sheets 002-97, 113-97, 115-97, and 064-97; interviews with USGS scientists Andy Lockhart, Ken McGee, John Ewert, Wendy McCausland, Seth Moran, John Pallister, Rowdy LeFevers, Julie Griswold, and Angie Diefenbach; Chilean scientists Luis Enrique Franco and Gonzalo Andrés Hermosilla; Indonesian scientists Supriyati Andreastuti, Dewi Sajuti, and Anjar Heriwaseso; and volcano observers Ismail and Purwono; and from site visits to CVO and Mount St. Helens National Monument, Mount Merapi Observatory in Yogyakarta, and the Babadan and Jrakah Observatories on Mount Merapi.

Selected Bibliography

Andreastuti, Supriyati, geologist with Balai Penyelidikan dan Pengembangan Teknologi Kegunungapian (BPPTK) the Center of Volcanology and Geological Hazard Mitigation (CVGHM), Volcanological Survey of Indonesia (VSI). In-person interviews with author, 2011.

Belford, Aubrey. "Indonesia Struggles After Tsunami and Volcano," *New York Times,* October 27, 2010.

Belford, Aubrey, and Will Carless. "Newer Eruption Drives More Indonesians to Shelter," *New York Times,* November 1, 2010.

Belton, David. *Volcano's Deadly Warning*. NOVA, 2003.

Bruce, Victoria. *No Apparent Danger: The True Story of Volcanic Disaster at Galeras and Nevado del Ruiz*. New York: HarperCollins, 2001.

Cascades Volcano Observatory. vulcan.wr.usgs.gov.

Cholis, Pak Nur, Balai Penyelidikan dan Pengembangan Teknologi Kegunungapian (BPPTK), the Center of Volcanology and Geological Hazard Mitigation (CVGHM), Volcanological Survey of Indonesia (VSI). In-person interviews with author, 2011.

Couchman, Marvin, technician, Volcano Disaster Assistance Program. In-person interviews with the author, 2010 and 2011.

Diefenbach, Angie, geologist, Volcano Disaster Assistance Program. In-person interviews with the author, 2011.

Driedger, Carolyn, Dan Dzurisin, Cynthia Gardner, Ken McGee, Seth Moran, and Jim Vallance, volcanologists, Cascades Volcano Observatory, United States Geological Survey. In-person interviews with the author, 2005–6.

Ewert, John, geologist, Volcano Disaster Assistance Program, and Scientists-in-Charge, Cascades Volcano Observatory, USGS. In-person interview with the author, 2010–11.

Ewert, John, Andy Lockhart, Jeff and Marvin Couchman. "The Volcano Disaster Assistance Program." Mount St. Helens Volcano Views & Brews presentation, 2009.

Ewert, John, Dan Miller, James W. Hendley III, and Paul Stauffer. "Mobile Response Teams Saves Lives in Volcano Crises." USGS Fact Sheet 064-97. 1998.

Franco, Luis Enrique, geologist with the Chilean Servicio Nacional de Geología y Minería (National Geology and Mining Service). In-person interview with the author, July 2010.

Griswold, Julie, geologist, Volcano Disaster Assistance Program. In-person interviews with the author, 2011.

Heriwaseso, Anjar, geologist with Balai Penyelidikan dan Pengembangan Teknologi Kegunungapian (BPPTK) Balai Penyelidikan dan Pengembangan Teknologi Kegunungapian (BPPTK) the Center of Volcanology and Geological Hazard Mitigation (CVGHM), Volcanological Survey of Indonesia (VSI). In-person interviews with author, 2011.

Hermosilla, Gonzalo Andrés, geologist with the Chilean Servicio Nacional de Geología y Minería (National Geology and Mining Service). In-person interview with the author, July 2010.

Ismail, observer, Babadan Observatory on Mount Merapi. In-person interview with the author, May 2011.

Lauber, Patricia. *Volcano: The Eruption and Healing of Mount St. Helens.* New York: Aladdin, 1986.

LeFevers, Martin (Rowdy), geologist, Volcano Disaster Assistance Program. In-person interviews with the author, 2010–11.

Lindop, Laurie. *Probing Volcanoes.* Brookfield, CT: Millbrook Press, 2003.

Lockhart, Andy, geophysicist, Volcano Disaster Assistance Program. In-person interviews with the author, 2010-2011.

McCausland, Wendy, seismologist, Volcano Disaster Assistance Program, in-person interviews with the author, 2010–11.

Myers, Bobbie, Steven R. Brantley, Peter R. Stauffer, and James W. Hendley II. "What Are Volcano Hazards?" UGSG Fact Sheet 002-97. 2004.

Newhall, Chris, James W. Hendley II, and Peter Stauffer. "Benefits of Volcano Monitoring Far Outweigh Costs." USGS Fact Sheet 115-97. 1998.

———. "The Cataclysmic 1991 Eruption of Mount Pinatubo, Philippines." USGS Fact Sheet 113-97. 1998.

"New Volcanic Eruption Sends Indonesians Fleeing." CNN Wire, Staff: October 30, 2010.

Pallister, John, geologist and director, Volcano Disaster Assistance Program. Interviews with the author, 2005–6, 2010, and 2011.

Purwono, observer, Jrakah Observatory on Mount Merapi. In-person interviews with the author, May 2011.

Quiano, Kathy. "Death Toll, Evacuations Rise After Indonesian Volcano Erupts." CNN, October 27, 2010.

"Residents Evacuated as Indonesian Volcano Rumbles." Associated Press, October 26, 2010.

Rusch, Elizabeth. *Will It Blow?: Become a Volcano Detective at Mount St. Helens.* Seattle: Sasquatch Books, 2007.

Sayudi, Dewi Sri, geologist with Balai Penyelidikan dan Pengembangan Teknologi Kegunungapian (BPPTK), the Center of Volcanology and Geological Hazard Mitigation (CVGHM), Volcanological Survey of Indonesia (VSI). In-person interviews with the author, 2011.

Scarth, Alwyn. *Vulcan's Fury: Man Against Volcano.* New Haven, CT: Yale University Press, 1999.

Smithsonian National Museum of Natural History, Global Volcanism Program, Volcanoes of the World, www.volcano.si.edu/world.

Subandrio, Pak, director of Balai Penyelidikan dan Pengembangan Teknologi Kegunungapian (BPPTK), the Center of Volcanology and Geological Hazard Mitigation (CVGHM), Volcanological Survey of Indonesia (VSI). In-person interviews with the author, 2011.

Thompson, Dick. *Volcano Cowboys: The Rocky Evolution of a Dangerous Science.* New York: St. Martin's Press, 2000.

USGS Volcano Hazards Program, volcanoes.usgs.gov.

USGS Volcano Disaster Assistance Program,

Voight, Barry. "The 1985 Nevado del Ruiz Volcano Catastrophe: Anatomy and Retrospection," *Journal of Volcanology and Geothermal Research,* 44, no. 3–4 (1990): 349–86.

volcanoes.usgs.gov/vdap/index.php; vulcan.wr.usgs.gov/Vdap/framework.html.

Index